●●● architecture in context

First published 1997 by
Könemann Verlagsgesellschaft mbH
Bonner Straße 126
D–50968 Köln

ISBN 3–89508–268–6 Könemann

Published in Asia by
Page One Publishing Pte Ltd
Block 4 Pasir Panjang Road
#06-35 Alexandra Distripark
Singapore 118491

ISBN 981-00-8409-9

Published in the UK by
●●●ellipsis london limited
55 Charlotte Road
London EC2A 3QT

ISBN 1–899858–22–9 ellipsis

Designed and produced by
●●●ellipsis london limited

Photography by Keith Collie
Text by Noriyuki Tajima and
Catherine Powell
Drawings by Micha Manz
Translated into German by
Andreas Klatt
Translated into French by
Armelle Tardiveau

Printed and bound in China

Tokyo

●●●architecture in context

labyrinth city

Noriyuki Tajima

Catherine Powell

photographs by

Keith Collie

●●●ellipsis **KÖNEMANN**

The experience of the city has been a significant part of many civilisations. Wandering within the densely packed environment of the city's boundaries, the traveller encounters an extraordinary variety of objects and people, experiencing and absorbing a discontinuous chain of impressions.

The city of Tokyo, perhaps more than any other, is constantly re-forming, adopting new and ever-changing directions. It presents the wanderer with a bewildering array of architecture – simultaneously rich, diverse and discordant – much of which has been built within the twentieth century. Widely divergent styles and scales co-exist side by side among a confusing clutter of signs, vending machines and transport networks.

In streets with so much to read, at times the environment seems indecipherable.

With its fast-changing history and endless movement, Tokyo can be explored as a labyrinthine narrative. Architecture is just one element among the multifarious urban phenomena that make up the complex city fabric. Even when a building is designed to be wholly autonomous, it inevitably becomes part of the involved melting pot of the city, a character within a story through which we can gain an insight into the sociological, cultural, political and philosophical issues that lie beneath the surface. Within the diverse cast of individuals and inhabitants who shape the city, the architect's vision takes its place and becomes one of the driving forces that cause it to

change direction, stimulating and giving rise to new concepts of 'cityness'.

This book presents four recent architectural episodes, each representative of a different issue within the context of the city of Tokyo.

The Sumida Culture Factory, a downtown community centre by Itsuko Hasegawa, explores the impact of mass-media culture on the local inhabitants. The issues of community access to and participation in both traditional culture and the latest media technology, and how these can interrelate, are contained within its fabric and design.

Patios 11, by Steven Holl, is a residential complex located just outside the capital in a newly developing satellite town. It is here, at the edge of the city, that land undergoes

the greatest changes and that planners and architects may experiment most freely with new visions of the city. The issue of commuter space and the phenomenon of the modern nomad also become topical.

Lars Bil, a residential and office building by Takeo Kimura and Tao Architects, draws its inspiration from the brazenly chaotic appearance of the contemporary cityscape. Trends that are commonly seen as negative – the shoulder-to-shoulder co-existence of old and new, of small scale and large, and the complete abandonment of any unifying design expression – are transformed into positive qualities.

The final building, the Fuji-Sankei Communications Group (FCG) headquarters by Kenzo Tange, illustrates how bureaucracy

Vivre la ville est un élément important pour nombre de civilisations. En errant dans le paysage dense de l'enceinte de la ville, le promeneur rencontre une variété extraordinaire d'objets et de gens; il découvre et s'imprègne d'une série d'impressions discontinues.

Cela est peut-être encore plus vrai pour Tokyo, ville en constante mutation, aux orientations sans cesse renouvelées. La ville offre au promeneur une extraordinaire palette architecturale à la fois diverse, variée et discordante dont la majeure partie a été construite au cours du XXème siècle. Les styles et les proportions les plus opposés cohabitent au milieu d'une cohue déroutante de panneaux, de distributeurs automatiques et de réseaux de transport. Il y a tant à lire

dans les rues que l'ensemble en devient parfois indéchiffrable.

Avec son histoire qui évolue très vite, comme un mouvement perpétuel, la ville de Tokyo peut-être lue comme une suite de dédales. L'architecture n'est qu'un élément parmi les phénomènes variés qui constituent le tissu urbain complexe de la ville. Même si un bâtiment est conçu de manière complèment autonome, il finira par s'intégrer à la diversité ambiante de la ville, comme le personnage d'une histoire grâce auquel on découvre les valeurs sociologique, culturelle, politique et philosophique qui effleurent la surface de la ville. Au milieu de cette diversité de gens et d'habitants qui représente bien la ville de Tokyo, la perception de l'architecte devient l'une des forces motrices qui

Das »Erlebnis Stadt« hat in vielen Zivili-sationen eine wichtige Rolle gespielt. Auf einem Spaziergang durch den dicht bebauten städtischen Raum trifft der Besucher auf eine außerordentliche Vielfalt an Objekten und Menschen; er erlebt und erfaßt eine dis-kontinuierliche Kette von Eindrücken.

Mehr als vielleicht jede andere Stadt ist Tokio laufend in einem Umbildungs-prozeß begriffen, schlägt neue und ständig wechselnde Richtungen ein. Tokio bietet dem Besucher ein verwirrendes und zugleich reiches, vielfältiges und widersprüchliches Aufgebot an Architektur – vieles davon aus dem 20. Jahrhundert. Grundverschiedene Stile und Maßstäbe stehen Seite an Seite inmitten eines konfusen Wirrwarrs aus Schildern, Automaten und Verkehrsnetzen.

In Straßen, wo es so viel zu sehen gibt, scheint die Umgebung mitunter unentwirrbar geworden zu sein.

Man kann Tokio, mit seiner schnellebigen Geschichte und seiner Rastlosigkeit, wie eine labyrinthische Erzählung erforschen. Die Architektur ist nur ein Element unter den vielgestaltigen Phänomenen, aus denen sich die komplexe Bausubstanz der Stadt zusammensetzt. Selbst wenn ein Gebäude vom Entwurf her als vollkommen autonom konzipiert ist, fließt es unweigerlich in den komplizierten Schmelztiegel der Stadt ein, wird zu einer Figur in einer Erzählung, durch die wir Einblick in die soziologischen, kultur-ellen, politischen und philosophischen Fragen gewinnen können, die unter der Oberfläche liegen. Zwischen den zahllosen Individuen, die

die Stadt gestalten, nimmt auch der Architekt seinen Platz ein; seine Vision wird zu einer treibenden Kraft, die Richtungswechsel hervorruft und neue Konzepte der »Stadt-artigkeit« anregt und aufkommen läßt.

Dieses Buch enthält vier neuere archi-tektonische Episoden, jede stellt eine andere Problematik im Kontext Tokios dar.

Die Kulturfabrik Sumida, ein inner-städtisches Gemeindezentrum von Architektin Itsuko Hasegawa, befaßt sich mit den Aus-wirkungen der Kultur der Massenmedien auf die Anwohner. Die Fragen des gemein-schaftlichen Zugangs zu und der Beteiligung an traditioneller Kultur sowie der neuesten Medientechnologie, aber auch deren Wechsel-wirkung, sind in Entwurf und Realisierung verkörpert.

Introduction

and politics play a role in shaping the cityscape. The building is situated on newly reclaimed land that was earmarked for an ambitious city exhibition and the creation of an international information-intensive bayside development. But the citizens of Tokyo, weary of schemes conceived in the now-discredited economic 'bubble' era of the 1980s, pulled the plug on the developers and their supporters in the metropolitan government and the scheme foundered. While the debate continues, we show one of the buildings that survived the turmoil, as yet unfinished.

Our aim within this book is to place architecture within a social, political and cultural framework, to raise awareness of the connections between architectural design and its context. The text is compiled from interviews with the architects, the authors' impressions, and written sources. Following the mood of the city, these essays and photographs can be read as fragments of the discourses and objects that together weave the labyrinthine narrative that is Tokyo.

---

engendrent les changements d'orientation, activant et donnant naissance à de nouveaux concepts de la ville.

Ce livre propose quatre épisodes d'architecture contemporaine, chacun d'eux illustrant un élément différent à l'intérieur de la ville de Tokyo.

L'Usine Culturelle de Sumida, un centre de quartier de Itsuko Hasegawa qui explore l'impact de la culture des médias sur les habitants du quartier. Les problèmes d'accès de la communauté et de sa participation tant à la culture traditionnelle qu'aux derniers moyens technologiques et comment ils s'intriquent et s'intègrent dans son tissu et son concept.

Patios 11 de Steven Holl est un ensemble résidentiel en périphérie de la capitale, dans une ville satellite en cours d'aménagement. C'est ici, à la limite de la ville, que le paysage subit les changements les plus importants et où urbanistes et architectes vont pouvoir expérimenter le plus librement possible de nouveaux concepts urbains. Le problème de l'espace du banlieusard et du phénomène de migration moderne sont au centre des préoccupations.

Lars Bill, un immeuble de logements et de bureaux de Takeo Kimura et Tao Architects, est inspiré de l'aspect effrontément chaotique du paysage urbain contemporain. Les mouvances, souvent négatives, deviennent ici des qualités positives: Apposition côte à côte d'ancien et de nouveau, de petite et grande échelle, et abandon total de tout signe donnant un sens d'unité.

Enfin, le siège social de Fuji-Sankei Communication Group, réalisé par Kenzo Tange, illustre le rôle que jouent la bureaucratie et la politique dans la composition du paysage urbain. Le bâtiment est situé sur un terrain qui a été récemment pris sur la mer et qui, à l'origine, aurait dû accueillir une importante exposition sur la ville ainsi que la création d'un centre de communication international sur le bord de mer. Mais lassés des projets conçus sous l'ère du «bubble» (bulles) des années 80 et aujourd'hui contestée, les habitants de Tokyo ont court-circuité les promoteurs et leurs partisans au sein de la municipalité si bien que le projet est parti en poussière. Alors que le débat à ce sujet se poursuit, nous présentons un des bâtiments qui a survécu à la tempête mais qui n'est pas encore terminé.

L'objectif de ce livre est de replacer l'architecture dans son contexte social, politique et culturel, et de mettre l'accent sur les liens qui existent entre le concept architectural et son environnement. Le texte est constitué d'interviews avec les architectes, des impressions des auteurs et d'articles parus dans la presse. Imprégnés de l'ambiance de la ville, ces textes/essais et photographies peuvent se lire comme des fragments d'autant de discours et d'objets qui, ensemble, alimentent cette suite de dédales que forme Tokyo.

Bei Patios 11 von Steven Holl handelt es sich um einen Wohnkomplex unweit der Metropole in einer noch entstehenden Satellitenstadt. Hier, am Stadtrand, erfährt das Land die größten Veränderungen; hier können Planer und Architekten besonders ungehemmt mit neuen Vorstellungen von der Stadt experimentieren. Die Frage des Aufenthaltsorts von Pendlern und das Phänomen des modernen Nomaden gehören ebenfalls hierin.

Lars Bil, ein Wohn- und Bürogebäude von Takeo Kimura und Tao Architects, bezieht seine Inspiration vom ausgeprägt chaotischen Erscheinungsbild der städtischen Landschaft von heute. Aus Trends, die allgemein als negativ gesehen werden – die dichtgedrängte Koexistenz von Alt und Neu, von Klein und Groß und der völlige Verzicht auf jedweden verbindenden Designanspruch –, werden positive Eigenschaften.

Als letztes Beispiel zeigt der Hauptsitz der Fuji-Sankei Communications Group von Kenzo Tange, welche Rolle Bürokratie und Politik bei der Gestaltung des Stadtbilds spielen. Das Gebäude wurde auf neu gewonnenem Land errichtet, das für eine ehrgeizige städtische Ausstellung und die Schaffung eines internationalen, vernetzten Bauprojekts am Ufer der Bucht vorgesehen war. Aber die Bürger Tokios waren der während der inzwischen diskreditierten »Konjunkturblase« der 80er Jahre entstandenen Projekte überdrüssig und drehten den Bauherren und deren Freunden in der Stadtverwaltung den Hahn ab; das Projekt scheiterte. Die Debatte wird jedoch weitergeführt, und wir zeigen ein – noch unfertiges – Gebäude, das die Wirren überlebt hat.

In diesem Buch soll die Architektur in einen sozialen, politischen und kulturellen Zusammenhang gesetzt werden, um auf diese Weise die Beziehungen zwischen dem architektonischen Entwurf und seinem Kontext bewußter zu machen. Zum Text haben Interviews mit den Architekten, die Eindrücke der Autoren und schriftliche Quellen beigetragen. Läßt man sich von der Stimmung dieser Stadt anregen, könnte man die Essays und Fotografien als Fragmente der Diskurse und Objekte sehen, die gemeinsam die labyrinthische Erzählung »Tokio« ausmachen.

As you turn a corner off a traffic-laden thoroughfare that runs through the downtown Sumida district of eastern Tokyo, you enter Higashi Mukojima. This area still resonates with the Edo lifestyle and traditions. Unlike other parts of Tokyo, where office developments have moved in and the locals have been forced to move out to the suburbs, people here still mostly live and work within the locality. Small family-owned industries, traditional crafts and a strong sense of community have survived.

Architect Itsuko Hasegawa: 'It was surprising to discover the extent to which the local inhabitants are still connected to Edo customs. They maintain all the traditional arts and festivals – to people from western Tokyo, they are like some kind of ancient fossil. But

it was also striking how positive and eager they are about the latest media technology and how they want to combine this with traditional communal activities. Life may be very local here, but their thoughts, by contrast, are very open.'

When we first visited the Sumida Culture Factory, Hasegawa's new community centre in Sumida district, all we had seen was the model. This featured a sphere and a series of repeated triangular forms at roof level that recalled the figurative elements which dominated the design of her Shonandai Culture Centre, where she used silver 'trees' and two cosmic spheres to create what she characterises as an 'artificial landscape'. Standing before the finished building, however, any anticipated sense of similarity

between the two schemes evaporated. Although the Sumida Culture Factory is also composed of many articulated parts, the materiality of the architecture takes a background role. Here, the movement of people from space to space within the building is strikingly revealed from the outside, while within, the interior is animated by light.

Mass-media culture forms part of Tokyo's urban landscape to a degree that could be called extreme. An insatiable appetite for the new, the different and the updated pervades the city. The origins of this obsession can be traced to the Edo period (1600–1867) when a system for disseminating information throughout the urban population was developed. In his essay 'The Origins of

Japanese Mass Culture' (The Electric Geisha, 1994), Takao Yoshii describes how the value systems of the townspeople, a newly arrived, mixed population, were in a state of constant flux and how 'the spread of information stimulated the creation of new common values … In the urban setting, social and cultural phenomena would arise one after another and each new value thus generated might soon be overturned by the next.' In its role as a media centre, the Sumida Culture Factory can be seen as a microcosm of the greater media city. Access, generation and transfer are integrated into its form and disseminated through its screen-like surfaces.

The sense of ephemerality contained within and projected by the fabric of Tokyo can be

Sitôt sorti del la rue encombrée qui traverse le quartier du centre de Sumida situé à l'est de Tokyo, vous pénétrez dans Higashi Mukojima. Ce quartier est encore imprégné du style de vie et des traditions Edo. Contrairement à d'autres quartiers de Tokyo où les bureaux ont investi les immeubles et donc forcé les habitants à émigrer du quartier et s'installer en banlieue. Ici, les gens vivent et travaillent encore dans le voisinage. Les petites entreprises familiales, les artisans tout comme le sens aigu d'appartenance à une communauté ont survécu au temps.

L'architecte Itsuko Hasegawa raconte: «Il est surprenant de voir à quel point les habitants du quartier sont toujours attachés à la tradition du Edo. Ils maintiennent les

arts traditionnels et les festivals. Les habitants de l'ouest de Tokyo les regardent presque comme s'ils étaient de vieux fossiles. Mais il est encore plus surprenant de voir à quel point ils s'intéressent et sont avides des technologies les plus récentes et combien ils les intègrent aux activités traditionnelles. Leur vie est peut-être cantonnée au quartier mais leur façon de penser, en revanche, est très ouverte.»

Lorsque nous nous sommes rendus à l'Usine Culturelle de Sumida, le nouveau centre du quartier de Sumida, conçu par Hasegawa, nous n'avions vu jusque-là que la maquette. Celle-ci représentait une sphère avec une série de formes triangulaires au niveau du toit rappelant les éléments figuratifs qui caractérisent la conception

Wenn man von der verkehrsreichen Durch-fahrtsstraße abbiegt, die den innerstäd-tischen Bezirk Sumida im Osten Tokios durchquert, kommt man nach Higashi Mukojima. In diesem Viertel sind Lebensstil und Traditionen des Edo noch lebendig. Im Gegensatz zu anderen Teilen Tokios, wo Gewerbebetriebe die Anwohner in die Rand-gebiete verdrängt haben, leben und arbeiten die meisten Menschen hier in der Nach-barschaft. Kleine Familienbetriebe, das traditionelle Handwerk und ein starkes Gemeinschaftsgefühl haben überlebt.

Dazu Architektin Itsuko Hasegawa: »Es war überraschend festzustellen, wie weit die Anwohner noch an den Sitten des Edo festhalten. Sie pflegen alle traditionellen Künste, begehen die Feste – den Menschen

aus dem Westen Tokios kommen sie wie ur-alte Fossilien vor. Aber es war auch auffällig, wie positiv und begeistert sie der neuesten Medientechnologie gegenüberstehen und sie mit traditionellen, gemeinschaftlichen Ak-tivitäten verbinden wollen. Das Leben hier mag zwar in engen Grenzen ablaufen, aber vom Denken her sind sie sehr offen.«

Als wir zum ersten Mal die Kulturfabrik Sumida besuchten, Hasegawas neues Gemein-dezentrum, hatten wir vorher nur das Modell gesehen. Es zeigte eine Kugel und eine Reihe von Dreiecksformen auf Dachhöhe; wir fühlten uns an die gegenständlichen Elemente er-innert, die ihren Entwurf für das Kulturzen-trum in Shonandai beherrschten. Damals hatte sie silberne »Bäume« und zwei kos-mische Sphären verwendet, um etwas zu

kreieren, das sie als »künstliche Landschaft« bezeichnete. Als wir jedoch vor dem fertigen Gebäude standen, schwand jeder vorgefaßte Eindruck einer Ähnlichkeit zwischen den beiden Projekten. Obwohl die Kulturfabrik Sumida ebenfalls aus vielen zusammen-hängenden Teilen besteht, tritt das Materielle der Architektur in den Hintergrund. Hier ist die Bewegung der Menschen im Inneren des Gebäudes von einem Raum zum anderen für die Außenwelt verblüffend sichtbar, während der Innenraum durch Licht zum Leben er-weckt wird.

Die Kultur der Massenmedien tritt im städtischen Erscheinungsbild Tokios in fast schon extremem Maße zutage. Die Stadt ist erfüllt von einem unstillbaren Drang nach allem, was neu, anders und aktuell ist. Den

Media screens

linked to the aesthetic of mujo – a state of no constancy, of mutability – found in traditional Japanese art forms. In Noh drama, for instance, the body is a changing surface on which the actors' gestures and attitudes are displayed in an indirect expression of the subject. The city and its structures take on a similar role to the stage sets and actors' bodies in Noh – they are the transient media on which temporary encounters are played out.

NT I noticed that the translucent quality of the wrapping – perforated aluminium panels – makes the activities of the people inside the Sumida centre look different than if they were seen through glass.

IH Yes, it is different. Movement becomes more apparent. Transparent glass reveals everything, not just movement, whereas translucency gives an impression of projected, shadowy movements.

NT The façade then becomes a kind of television screen, doesn't it?

IH Oh, yes, but black and white.

du centre culturel de Shonandai où l'architecte a employé des «arbres» argentés et deux sphères cosmiques pour créer ce qu'elle appelle «un paysage artificiel». Cependant, une fois devant le bâtiment réalisé, toute idée de similarité que l'on aurait pu imaginer entre les deux projets disparaît. Bien que l'Usine Culturelle de Sumida soit composée de nombreux éléments articulés, la matérialité de l'architecture passe au second plan. Ici, le mouvement des gens qui vont d'un espace à l'autre du bâtiment se perçoit clairement depuis le dehors tandis qu'à l'intérieur, c'est la lumière qui anime le lieu.

La culture des médias fait partie intégrante du paysage urbain de Tokyo à un degré que l'on pourrait qualifier d'extrême. Un appétit insatiable pour le nouveau, le différent et la dernière nouveauté a envahi la ville. On retrouve l'origine de cette obsession dans la période Edo (1900–1867), époque où un système permettant la diffusion d'informations au sein de la population urbaine fut développé. Dans un essai intitulé «Les origines de la culture de masse japonaise» (The Electric Geisha, 1994), Takao Yoshii décrit comment les systèmes de valeurs des citadins – une population mélangée et installée là depuis peu – étaient en perpétuel mouvement et comment «la diffusion de l'information a favorisé la création de nouvelles valeurs communes… Dans l'environnement urbain, les phénomènes sociaux et culturels émergeaient les uns après les autres et chaque nouvelle valeur créée pouvait aussitôt écarter la précédente.» Avec son rôle de centre des médias, l'Usine Culturelle de Sumida peut être considérée comme un microcosme de la ville des médias. Accès, création et circulation font partie intégrante de la structure et se répandent sur la surface du bâtiment telle un écran.

Le sens de l'éphémère qui émane du tissu urbain de Tokyo peut être mis en corrélation avec l'esthétique mujo – un état de fluctuation, de mutation – que l'on retrouve dans les formes formes traditionnelles de l'art japonais. Dans le théâtre Nô, par exemple, le corps est compris comme une surface changeante sur laquelle la gestuelle et les mouvements des comédiens manifestent une expression indirecte du sujet. La ville et sa structure jouent un rôle semblable à celui de la scène et du corps des acteurs de Nô – ils sont les médias transitoires sur lesquels s'opèrent des rencontres éphémères.

NT J'ai remarqué que l'aspect translucide de l'enveloppe – faite de panneaux d'aluminium perforés – fait que l'activité des gens qui se trouvent à l'intérieur du centre se perçoit autrement que s'ils étaient vus à travers une paroi de verre.

IH En effet, c'est différent. Le mouvement devient apparent. Le verre transparent met tout à nu tandis que le verre translucide donne à voir des mouvements projetés, comme des ombres.

NT La façade devient-elle alors une sorte d'écran de télévision?

IH Oui, mais en noir et blanc.

Ursprung dieser Manie kann man bereits im Edo-Zeitalter (1600–1867) feststellen, als ein System zur Verbreitung von Informationen unter der Stadtbevölkerung entwickelt wurde. In seinem Essay »Die Ursprünge japanischer Massenkultur« (The Electric Geisha, 1994) beschreibt Takao Yoshii, wie sich das Wertesystem der Stadtbewohner, einer neu eingetroffenen, gemischten Bevölkerungsgruppe, ständig wandelte und wie »die Informationsverbreitung das Entstehen neuer, gemeinsamer Werte förderte … Im städtischen Kontext trat ein soziales und kulturelles Phänomen nach dem anderen auf, und jeder so entstandene neue Wert konnte schon bald vom nächsten wieder abgelöst werden.« Die Kulturfabrik Sumida kann in ihrer Rolle eines Medienzentrums als Mikrokosmos der grö-ßeren Medienstadt verstanden werden. Zugang, Erstellung und Vermittlung sind in ihre Form integriert und werden über ihre bildschirmartigen Flächen verbreitet.

Das Gefühl der Vergänglichkeit, das in der Bausubstanz Tokios enthalten ist und von dieser projiziert wird, läßt sich mit der Ästhetik des mujo – eines in den traditionellen japanischen Kunstformen anzutreffenden Zustands der Unbeständigkeit, des Wechselhaften – in Zusammenhang bringen. So gilt beispielsweise im No-Theater der Körper als eine sich wandelnde Fläche, auf der Gesten und Geisteshaltung der Schauspieler als indirekter Ausdruck des Themas zur Schau gestellt werden. Die Stadt und ihre Strukturen verkörpern eine ähnliche Rolle wie das Bühnenbild und die Körper der Schauspieler beim No – sie sind die vergänglichen Medien, in denen zeitlich begrenzte Begegnungen ablaufen.

NT Mir fiel auf, daß die Aktivitäten der Menschen im Sumida-Zentrum aufgrund der Lichtdurchlässigkeit der Verpackung – perforierte Aluminiumtafeln – anders aussehen, als wenn man sie durch Glas wahrnähme.

IH Ja, das ist anders. Die Bewegung wird deutlicher sichtbar. Transparentes Glas legt alles offen, nicht bloß Bewegung, während Lichtdurchlässigkeit den Eindruck projizierter, schattenhafter Bewegungen vermittelt.

NT Die Fassade wird dadurch zu einer Art Fernsehbildschirm, nicht wahr?

IH O ja, aber schwarzweiß.

Sumida Culture Factory
Itsuko Hasegawa Atelier

1

1 Viewed from the east, the dome
and triangular roof forms of
the Sumida Culture Factory
float above the traditional two-
storey buildings that characterise
the area.
2 The lucidity of the screen-like
façade contrasts with the visual
chaos of the traditional Tokyo
streetscape.

1 Vue de l'est, le dôme et les formes
triangulaires du toit de l'Usine
Culturelle de Sumida flottent au
dessus des bâtiments traditionnels
à deux étages qui caractérisent
le quartier.
2 La transparence de la façade,
telle un écran, contraste avec le
chaos d'ensemble de la silhouette
traditionnelle des rues de Tokyo.

1 Von Osten aus betrachtet
schweben die Kugel und die
Dreiecksformen der Kulturfabrik
Sumida über den Dächern der
zweistöckigen Gebäude, die diesen
Stadtteil beherrschen.
2 Die Helle der Fassade kontrastiert
mit dem visuellen Chaos des traditionellen Stadtbildes von Tokio.

1

1–2 The building's incongruity has
caused it to be compared to a
circus tent moored temporarily
in its urban setting.
3 The south elevation presents
a constantly changing display to
the street.

1–2 L'incongruité du bâtiment lui a
valu d'être comparé à un cirque
planté temporairement dans un
cadre urbain.
3 L'élevation sud donne à la rue un
aspect en mutation constante.

1–2 Fremdartig wie ein Zirkuszelt.
Das Gebäude scheint nur
vorübergehend im städtischen
Grau verankert zu sein.
3 Die Südseite präsentiert sich
dem Passanten in einem ständig
neuen Licht.

2

3

1

1–3 Both open spaces and the
glass structure are wrapped in
perforated aluminium screens
that give a sense of openness and
accessibility.

1–3 Les espaces ouverts et la structure
de verre sont enveloppés dans
des écrans en aluminium perforé
qui donnent une impression
d'ouverture et d'accessibilité.

1–3 Sowohl freie Räume als auch die
Glasstruktur sind in perforierte
Aluminiumbleche verpackt, die
ein Gefühl der Offenheit und
Zugänglichkeit vermitteln.

2

1 View from the west.
2 The desire for openness is
  carried through into the plan.
  The central plaza provides
  glimpses of activities in other
  parts of the building.

1 Vue côté ouest.
2 La volonté d'ouverture se poursuit
  à l'intérieur du plan. L'esplanade
  centrale permet une vue sur les
  activités dans les autres salles
  du bâtiment.

1 Blick von Westen.
2 Der Wunsch nach Offenheit
  hat sich in der Planung erfüllt.
  Die zentrale Piazza erschließt
  Momentaufnahmen vom Leben
  in anderen Teilen des Gebäudes.

1

2

1-4 The light stands in the central
plaza introduce unusual street
furniture.

1-4 Les éclairages indépendants de
l'esplanade centrale introduisent
un élément de mobilier de rue.

1-4 Leuchtkörper in der zentralen
Piazza.

4

1

1–2 Audio-visual space on the third
level. Translucent partitions
provide flexibility and allow
activities to overlap.
3–5 'Space-zone' foyer to the
planetarium on the fourth level.

1–2 Espace audio-visuel du troisième
niveau. Les cloisons translucides
permettent à la fois une certaine
flexibilité et un chevauchement
des activités.
3–5 «Zone-espace» foyer menant au
planétarium situé au quatrième
niveau.

1–2 AV-Räume in der dritten Etage.
Leuchtende Raumteiler bieten
Flexibilität und gestatten eine
Überlappung der Raumnutzung.
3–5 »Raumzone« als Eingang zum
Planetarium in der vierten Etage.

2

3

4

5

1–9 Rooftop details. The two wings of the building are connected by nine bridges as well as open hallways and staircases.

1–9 Détail du toit. Les deux ailes du bâtiments sont reliées par neuf ponts ainsi que par des passerelles ouvertes et des escaliers.

1–9 Dachdetails. Die beiden Flügel sind durch neun Brücken, offene Gänge und Treppen miteinander verbunden.

Sumida Culture Factory

5

6

7

8

9

The sudden appearance of a vast, translucent, glowing mass of volumes in a drab neighbourhood of narrow twisting lanes and shabby two-storey buildings is astonishing. Swathes of perforated aluminium screens act as a membrane, wrapping open spaces and a glass-covered structure. Its incongruity within its surroundings, extraordinary lightness and simple materials have caused Itsuko Hasegawa's Sumida Culture Factory to be likened to a circus tent tethered in a chaotic sea of urban greyness. In comparison with the dense cityscape around it, it expresses a softer order.

The local-authority client wanted a centre for cultural exchange and the dissemination of information to serve the local community. Although this basic programme has not been radically altered, Hasegawa was concerned about two factors. First, the local authority envisaged a scheme that would compartmentalise the many proposed activities into specially designated areas. This format would preclude the integration and crossover of activities, while the diverse range of functions and spaces would make the organisation of the centre chaotic. Second, despite an alleged aim of delegating the control of community activities into the hands of its members, close consultation with the potential users of the building had not been undertaken to any useful degree. Instead, the council had consulted a government think-tank.

Hasegawa initiated her own independent programme of investigation. She conceived of the building as made up of two integrated components: 'hardware' and 'software'. The hardware was the building itself and the software the users and functions. The programme for the software took shape over a four-year period through discussions with local drama groups, computer specialists, craftspeople, psychologists and councillors. It was Hasegawa's intention to find new ways to combine areas housing different activities which would be interconnected to form an 'agora of activity'. In effect the building became a factory sheltering a network of information and events.

The overall transparency of the building suggests open access for all. The users themselves become its subject and patterns of activity and movement can be followed from the street and from points inside. There are few solid walls or wholly enclosed spaces. Instead, the two wings are connected by nine bridges, open hallways and staircases. One wing houses more traditional activities such as sewing workshops, a pottery and *tatami* and meeting rooms while the other includes computer rooms, a library, audio-visual rooms, music studios and an amateur radio studio. A planetarium and theatre are located to the rear.

Because of the ground on which it is built, the bulk of the building had to be

L'apparition soudaine d'une masse de volumes immenses, translucides et rayonnants surprend au milieu de ce quartier morne aux rues étroites et tortueuses et aux immeubles délabrés de deux étages. La membrane, faite de bandes d'écrans en aluminium perforé emmaillote les espaces ouverts et la structure habillée de verre. Son incongruité avec le voisinage, son extraordinaire légèreté et la simplicité des matériaux employés font ressembler l'Usine Culturelle à un chapiteau d'un cirque planté dans une mer déchaînée de grisaille urbaine. Elle exprime un ordre plus harmonieux que celui du paysage dense qui l'entoure.

La municipalité, maître d'ouvrage, voulait un centre d'échange culturel et de

1 North end of the central plaza.
2 Entrance hall.
3 Furniture designed by the architect.

1 Côté nord de l'esplanade centrale.
2 Hall d'entrée.
3 Meubles dessinés par l'architecte.

1 Nordseite der zentralen Piazza.
2 Eingangshalle.
3 Möbel nach dem Entwurf der Architektin.

Die plötzliche Manifestation eines mächtigen, opak leuchtenden Kristallgewächses in einem tristen Stadtviertel mit engen, gewundenen Gassen und schäbigen, zweistöckigen Gebäuden verblüfft. Perforierte Aluminiumtafeln wirken wie eine Membran, umwickeln offene Flächen und eine verglaste Struktur. Aufgrund ihrer Fremdartigkeit in dieser Umgebung, ihrer vermeintlichen Schwerelosigkeit und der Schlichtheit der Materialien hat man die Kulturfabrik gelegentlich mit einem Zirkuszelt verglichen, verankert in einem wallenden Meer aus städtischem Grau in Grau. Verglichen mit dem undurchdringlichen Stadtpanorama kommt in ihr ein leichterer Charakter zum Ausdruck.

Der kommunale Bauherr hatte ur-

sprünglich ein Zentrum für Kulturaustausch und Information für die ortsansässige Bevölkerung gefordert. Obwohl dieses Grundkonzept keine radikale Änderung erfuhr, ging es der Architektin Itsuko Hasegawa vor allem um zwei Aspekte. Erstens hatte sich die Kommunalverwaltung ursprünglich vorgestellt, die vielerlei geplanten Aktivitäten räumlich zweckbestimmt zu streuen; doch ein solcher Ansatz hätte Integration und gegenseitige Wechselwirkung unmöglich gemacht und letztlich ein chaotisches Nebeneinander erzwungen. Zweitens war zwar die Rede von Dezentralisierung und zunehmender Selbstverantwortung der Bürger für die künftigen Veranstaltungen, aber sinnvolle Diskussionen mit den

eigentlichen Nutznießern der Einrichtung hatten kaum stattgefunden. Statt dessen hatte sich die Kommunalverwaltung von einer Expertenkommission der Regierung beraten lassen.

Hasegawa leitete eine eigene, unabhängige Untersuchung ein. Sie stellte sich ein Objekt aus zwei integrierten Komponenten vor: »Hardware« und »Software«. Unter Hardware war das Gebäude selbst zu verstehen, unter Software die Benutzer und Funktionen. Das Programm für die Software entstand über einen Zeitraum von vier Jahren in Beratungen mit Theatergruppen, Computerexperten, Handwerkern, Psychologen und Gemeinderatsmitgliedern. Hasegawa wollte neue Wege finden, um bestimmte Bereiche für

above street level. As a result it easily
overwhelms its neighbours, though this
is countered to some extent by its
transparency and the green area laid
out around it.

In the daytime the white spaces receive
sunlight through the translucent panels
and the interior responds to the changes of
light. Under certain conditions the layering
of translucency creates the illusion of a fine
mist. Furniture also designed by Hasegawa
provides vivid flashes of colour. During the
evening the interior lighting spills out into
the street. Light bounces off walls and
ceilings, while the perforated panels
provide a *shoji*-like effect.

diffusion d'informations pour la
communauté locale. Sans modifier le
cahier des charges, Hasegawa s'est
penchée sur deux points en particulier.
D'une part, la municipalité concevait
un projet qui aurait compartimenté les
différentes activités en des espaces assignés
tout spécifiquement. Cette solution aurait
eu l'inconvénient d'empêcher l'intégration
des activités tandis que la diversité
des fonctions et espaces auraient rendu
l'organisation du centre chaotique.
D'autre part, malgré la tentative de
délégation des activités locales aux mains
des habitants, aucune consultation avec
les utilisateurs potentiels n'a été entreprise;
en revanche, on a eu recours à un groupe
d'experts de la municipalité.

Hasegawa a donc mis en place son
propre programme de recherche. Elle
a conçu le bâtiment comme deux
composantes intégrées: «hardware» –
le bâtiment lui-même – et «software» – les
utilisateurs et les fonctions diverses.
Le programme du software est le résultat
de quatre années de discussions avec
des compagnies de théâtre locales, des
spécialistes en informatique, des artisans,
des psychologues et des conseillers
municipaux. Hasegawa a cherché de
nouvelles manières de relier entre eux les
espaces abritant des activités différentes
afin qu'ils forment une «agora des
activité». Le résultat est un bâtiment
transformé en une usine qui abrite un
réseau d'information et d'événements.

La transparence générale du bâtiment
suggère l'accès ouvert à tous. Les
utilisateurs en deviennent le sujet et les
motifs d'une activité et d'un mouvement
que l'on peut suivre de la rue et, par
endroits, depuis l'intérieur. Rares sont
les murs pleins et les espaces totalement
clos. Au lieu de cela, les deux ailes
sont reliées par des couloirs ouverts,
des escaliers et neufs ponts. Une aile abrite
des activités plus traditionnelles telles
que des ateliers de couture, de poterie, de
tatami et des salles de réunion. Une autre
aile est réservée aux salles d'informatique
et d'audiovisuel, aux studios de radio
et de musique et à la bibliothèque.
Le planétarium et le théâtre sont situés
à l'arrière du bâtiment.

Étant donné le terrain, il a fallu
rehaussé le corps principal du bâtiment
au-dessus du niveau de la rue. En
conséquence, celui-ci a tendance à écraser
les bâtiments voisins mais cet effet est
rééquilibré par la transparence de
l'immeuble et l'espace vert qui l'entoure.

Dans la journée, les espaces blancs sont
inondés de lumière grâce aux panneaux
translucides et l'intérieur réagit aux
changements de lumière. Parfois, la
composition de la translucidité crée une
illusion de brume légère. Le mobilier,
également conçu par Hasegawa, offre des
éclats de couleurs vives. Le soir, la lumière
intérieure du bâtiment illumine la rue et
les panneaux perforés donnent un effet
semblable au shoji.

einzelne Aktivitäten zu kombinieren und
zu einer »Agora der Aktivität« zu ver-
knüpfen. Aus dem Gebäude wurde tat-
sächlich eine Fabrik, die ein Netzwerk aus
Informationen und Veranstaltungen auf-
nimmt.

Durch die übergreifende Transparenz
des Gebäudes kommt der offene Zugang
für alle zum Ausdruck. Die Benutzer selbst
werden zum Thema; Aktivitäts- und Be-
wegungsmuster lassen sich von der Straße
und von bestimmten Stellen innerhalb des
Gebäudes aus verfolgen. Massive Wände
oder vollkommen umschlossene Flächen
gibt es kaum. Statt dessen werden die
beiden Flügel durch neun Brücken, offene
Gänge und Treppen miteinander verbunden. In einem Flügel stößt man eher

auf traditionelle Interessen, z. B. Näh-
kreise, eine Töpferwerkstatt, eine Tatami-
weberei, auch Sitzungsräume; im anderen
befinden sich Computerräume, eine Biblio-
thek, AV-Räume, Musikstudios und ein
Amateur-Funkstudio. Im hinteren Teil sind
ein Planetarium und ein Theater untergebracht.

Aufgrund des Standortes mußte sich
das Bauwerk stark über das Straßenniveau
erheben. Die Gefahr, daß benachbarte
Gebäude überschattet werden könnten,
wurde teils durch die Transparenz aufge-
wogen, teils aber auch durch die umlie-
genden Grünanlagen.

Tagsüber fällt Sonnenlicht durch die
lichtdurchlässigen Felder auf die weißen
Räume, und das Innere des Gebäudes

reagiert auf das Wechselspiel des Lichtes.
Unter bestimmten Bedingungen entsteht
durch die Schichtung der Lichtdurchlässigkeit eine Illusion von leichtem Nebel.
Die ebenfalls von Hasegawa entworfenen
Möbel setzen strahlende Farbakzente.
Abends wird die Straße vom Licht aus
dem Inneren des Gebäudes überflutet.
Das Licht wird von Wänden und Decken
reflektiert, während die perforierten Felder
einen shoji-Effekt schaffen.

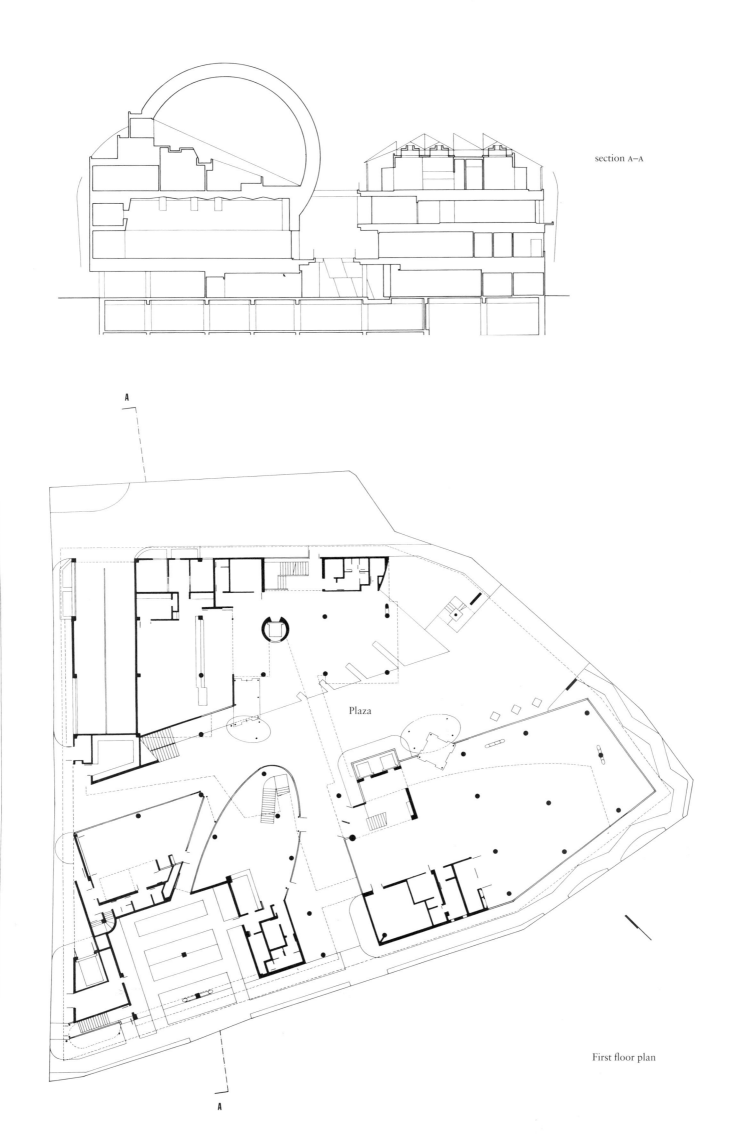

section A–A

A

Plaza

First floor plan

A

Itsuko Hasegawa Atelier
1994
Address 2-38-7 Higashi-mukojima
Sumida Ward, Tokyo
Client Sumida Ward
Contractor Ando; Higashi-Takeya-Uchida;
Tokyo Hasegawa Collaborations
Structure Umezawa Design Office
Site area 3400 square metres
Size 8448 square metres
Publications KENCHIKUBUNKA (1/93); GA JAPAN
(12/94); SHINKENCHIKU (1/95);
BAUWELT (2/95); ARCHITECTURAL
REVIEW (9/95); DETAIL (10/95);
AD (11/95); SD (11/95)

20 metres

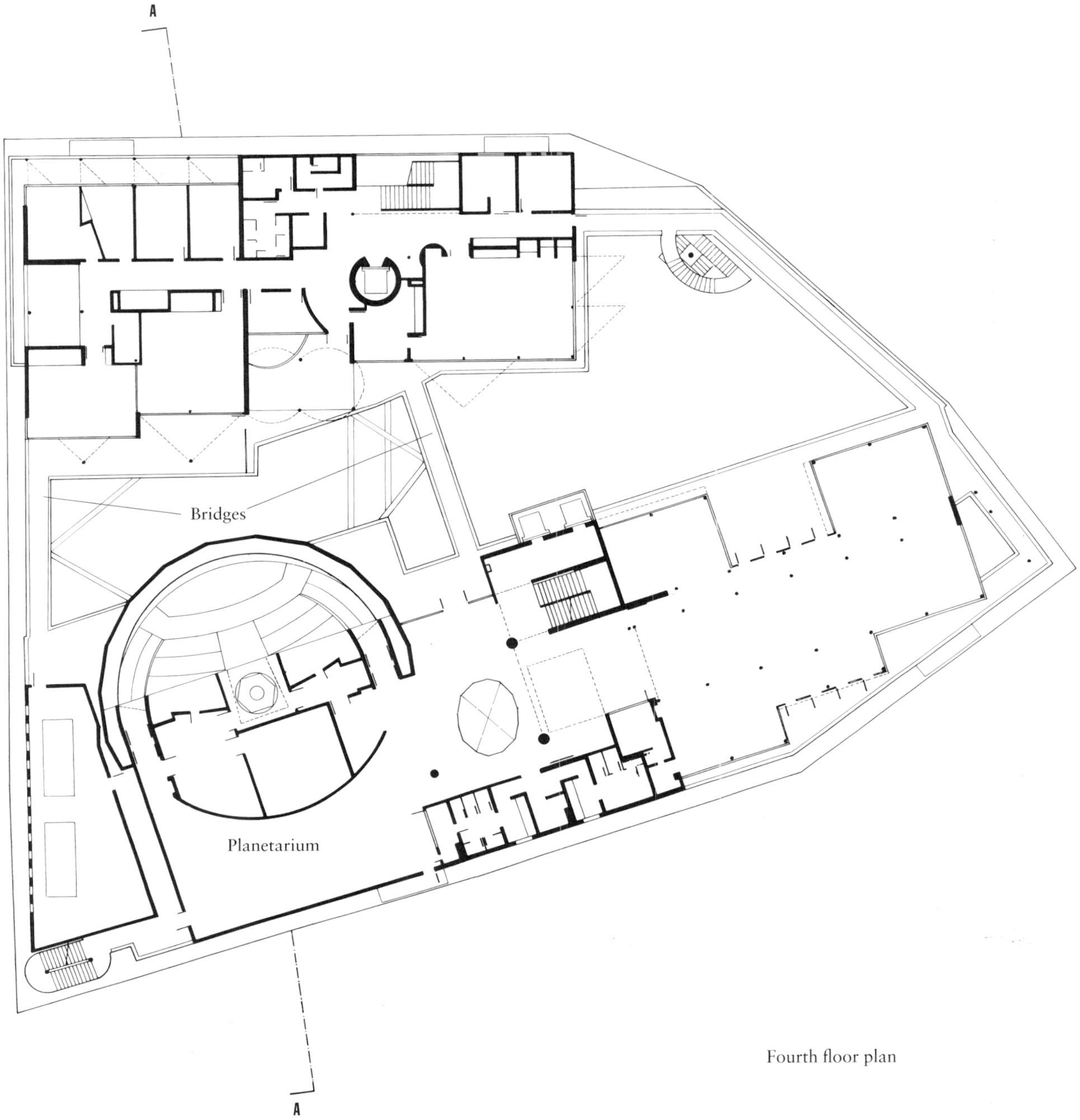

A

Bridges

Planetarium

Fourth floor plan

New Town Makuhari is located on reclaimed land beside Tokyo Bay, midway between central Tokyo and Narita International Airport (about 30 minutes from each). The development, supported by the local authority, will eventually be one of the largest in Japan, covering 522 hectares, with space and facilities for a projected 150,000 office workers and 26,000 inhabitants. The Makuhari Messe, a convention centre designed by Fumihiko Maki containing a vast 3100 square metre hall, is the centrepiece of the new city. 'Future City 2001', as the brochures call it, is intended to attract companies away from the chaotic, unplanned capital to its spacious, coherently laid-out avenues and gleaming glass-curtain-wall office blocks.

The most common Japanese word for city is toshi. The kanji character is a compound of the ancient word for city and the word for market. So the fortified towns of earlier times were conceived of in equal measure as a business district and a seat of government.

As we entered the new city from Tokyo, we were struck by the absence of the characteristic elements of the Japanese urban landscape. There were no flurries of people or untidy heaps of bicycles, no blinking neon signs or cable-draped poles. This is a Japanese city without the familiar sakariba (small shopping malls), the cacophony from pachinko parlours or the drifting smells from street food stalls. In their place is a sanitised pastiche of a western urban model.

Who lives here? The brochure features shots of Caucasians strolling through an unidentified American city, eating ice-cream and engaging in healthy activities. The front cover shows a pavement café somewhere in France. Although there are references to many cultures, the city belongs to none. As we headed back to Tokyo, the drawbacks of the 'prefabricate-and-lower-into-place' style of city building were apparent. Living in a 'rat's-nest' city took on a new glow.

The proliferation of suburban railways during this century has turned Tokyo into a megatropolis. A line is shot out to an area of land that has been bought up by the railway company, which then develops it with department stores, housing and facilities. The noodle-like tangle of the current train map is bewildering. In 1932 Tokyo spanned about 10 kilometres. By 1960 this had stretched to 30 kilometres. In 1975 its breadth had reached 60 kilometres, with an outer ring of developing satellite towns. Today the city's edge is increasingly difficult to detect, but its span is on the way to 100 kilometres. And new railway lines continue to open up – two in the past year alone. The growth shows no sign of abating.

The conditions for American architect Steven Holl's Patios 11 residential development in Makuhari recall those of his 'Edge of a City' project undertaken in the late 1980s. Here he explored the theory that 'to counter sprawl at the periphery of cities, the formation of spaces rather than the formation of objects is the primary aim.' Four visionary

La ville nouvelle de Makuhari est située sur un terrain pris sur mer de la Baie de Tokyo entre le centre de Tokyo et l'aéroport international de Narita (à 30 minutes de l'un ou l'autre). L'aménagement soutenu par la municipalité sera l'un des plus grands du Japon une fois terminé. Il couvre une surface de 522 hectares avec espaces et équipements pour une population active estimée à 150 000 employés et 26 000 habitants. Le Makuhari Messe est un centre de conférences qui est au coeur de la ville nouvelle. Conçu par Fumihiko Maki, il renferme un hall immense de 3 100 mètres carrés. Le «Future City 2001» comme l'appellent les brochures, a pour but d'attirer les entreprises de la capitale si chaotique et désordonnée, vers les grandes avenues, au dessin cohérent, bordées d'immeubles de bureaux scintillants avec murs-rideaux.

En japonais, le mot habituel pour ville est toshi. Le caractère chinois est composé du mot ancien pour ville et du mot marché. Ainsi, les villes fortifiées d'autrefois étaient conçues avec un quartier commerçant et un siège de gouvernement, chacun de proportion égale.

Venant de Tokyo, on est frappés en entrant dans la ville nouvelle, par l'absence des éléments propres au paysage urbanistique japonais. Il n'y a aucune activité humaine, pas de vélos entassés les uns sur les autres ni d'enseignes publicitaires qui clignotent ou encore moins de câbles accrochés aux poteaux. Voici une ville japonaise sans les traditionnelles sakariba (petites galeries marchandes), sans la cacophonie des salles

Makuhari ist eine Reißbrettstadt, die auf neu gewonnenem Land an der Bucht von Tokio entsteht, auf halbem Wege zwischen der Stadtmitte und dem internationalen Flughafen Narita (von beiden ca. 30 Minuten entfernt). Das von der Stadtverwaltung finanzierte Bauprojekt wird einmal zu den größten des Landes zählen; auf insgesamt 522 Hektar sollen hier Räumlichkeiten und Einrichtungen für voraussichtlich 150 000 Büroangestellte und 26 000 Anwohner entstehen. Die Makuhari-Messe, ein von Fumihiko Maki entworfenes Tagungszentrum mit einer riesigen, 3100 m² großen Halle, steht im Mittelpunkt der neuen Stadt. Dieses von den Werbebroschüren zur »Future City 2001« gekürte Projekt soll von der chaotischen, planlos angelegten Hauptstadt in ihre großzügigen, zweckmäßig angelegten Alleen und glitzernd verglasten Bürohäuser locken.

Das im Japanischen am häufigsten gebrauchte Wort für Stadt ist toshi. Das Schriftzeichen setzt sich aus dem uralten Wort für Stadt und dem Wort für Markt zusammen. Die befestigten Städte der Vergangenheit wurden also gleichermaßen als Geschäftsviertel und Verwaltungssitz gesehen.

Als wir von Tokio kommend die neue Stadt betraten, fiel uns auf, daß die typischen Elemente des japanischen Stadtbildes fehlten. Es gab weder hektische Passanten noch wirre Fahrradhaufen, weder blinkende Neonreklamen noch kabelstarke Masten. Hier war eine japanische Stadt ohne die vertrauen sakariba (kleine Einkaufspassagen), ohne die Kakophonie der Pachinko-Salons oder die Geruchswolken der Imbißbuden. An ihrer Stelle findet man die sanierte Nachahmung eines westlichen Stadtmodells.

Wer wohnt hier? In der Broschüre stößt man auf Fotos von Kaukasiern, die durch eine unbekannte amerikanische Stadt spazieren, Eis essen und gesundheitsfördernden Aktivitäten nachgehen. Auf dem Umschlag ist ein Straßencafé irgendwo in Frankreich abgebildet. Zwar wird auf viele Kulturen Bezug genommen, aber die Stadt gehört zu keiner. Als wir nach Tokio zurückfuhren, wurden die Nachteile dieses Städtebaustils à la »Fertighaus vom Kran« klar. Auf einmal schien es viel reizvoller, in einem »Rattennest« zu wohnen.

Durch den Bau einer Unzahl von Vorortbahnen im Laufe dieses Jahrhunderts ist Tokio

New place, new home

urban planning schemes for the outskirts of Dallas, Manhattan, Cleveland and Phoenix in the US were set out. Holl suggested that the creation of 'an intensified urban realm could be a coherent mediator between the extremes of the metropolis and the agrarian realm.'

At the time of writing, Patios 11 stands at the edge of the development, though it will soon be surrounded by further residential blocks. Each of these blocks has been designed by a different architect to achieve variety, though heights have been fixed and regular street façades stipulated. Despite the presence of a number of interesting schemes, the area has a suffocating feel. Although an opportunity to rethink the edge of the city existed, it seems that new approaches will remain in the plan chests.

de jeux et les parfums émanant des stands de nourriture. Au lieu de cela, on a une imitation du modèle urbain occidental.

Qui vit ici? La brochure présente des photos d'occidentaux qui se promènent dans une ville américaine non-identifiable en mangeant des glaces ou occupés à des activités sportives. Bien qu'on sente les références à différentes cultures, la ville n'appartient à aucune d'elles. Sur le chemin du retour à Tokyo, les désavantages des villes construites sur des immeubles préfabriqués avec des éléments incorporés nous apparaissent clairement. Vivre dans une ville grouillante nous semble soudain attrayant.

La multiplication des lignes de chemin de fer pour la banlieue, tout au long de ce siècle, a transformé Tokyo en une mégapole. On

trace une ligne de la parcelle de terrain que la compagnie de chemin de fer a acheté. Cette dernière peut alors y implanter des magasins, des logements et des équipements divers. L'actuel plan du réseau ferroviaire, pareil à un plat de nouilles, est déroutant. En 1932, Tokyo s'étendait sur plus de 10 kilomètres. En 1960, la ville s'était étirée sur 30 kilomètres et en 1975, elle faisait 60 kilomètres de large avec un boulevard périphérique au-delà duquel se développent des villes nouvelles. Aujourd'hui, il est extrêmement difficile de délimiter la ville, mais on peut estimer qu'elle s'étend sur quelque 100 kilomètres. On continue d'inaugurer de nouvelles lignes de train – ne serait-ce que l'année passée, on en a ouvert deux. Et rien n'indique que son accroissement ne va pas ralentir.

Les conditions de l'aménagement résidentiel du Patios 11 par l'architecte américain Steven Holl rappellent celles de son projet intitulé «Limite de la Ville» entrepris à la fin des années 80. Ici, il met en pratique la théorie selon laquelle «la création d'espaces plutôt que d'objets est essentielle pour parer à l'étalement urbain à la périphérie des villes». Il a dessiné quatre études urbanistiques projetées sur les périphéries de Dallas, Manhattan, Cleveland et Phoenix aux États Unis. Selon Holl, la création d'un «univers urbain rendu plus dense pourrait servir d'intermédiaire entre les extrêmes des mégapoles et l'univers agricole».

Au moment de la rédaction de cet essai, Patios 11 jouxte un aménagement entouré de terrain non construits mais qui sera bientôt

investi par des immeubles de logements. Chacun de ces immeubles a été conçu par un architecte différent pour offrir une certaine variété, même si la hauteur des immeubles et l'alignement des façades ont été imposés par les urbanistes. Malgré un certain nombre de projets intéressants, le quartier a quelque chose d'étouffant. Bien que l'occasion de redéfinir les abords de la ville se soit présentée, il semble que ces nouvelles idées resteront au placard.

zu einer Megatropole geworden. Man baut eine Strecke zu einem Stück Land hinaus, das von der Bahngesellschaft aufgekauft worden ist und dann von ihr mit Kaufhäusern, Wohnungen und sonstigen Einrichtungen bebaut wird. Beim Blick auf die Landkarte verliert man sich in einem Spaghettinetz von Strecken. Im Jahre 1932 erstreckte sich Tokio über etwa zehn Kilometer. 1960 waren es bereits 30 Kilometer. 1975 hatte die Stadt einen Durchmesser von 60 Kilometern, und ein äußerer Ring von Satellitenstädten befand sich im Bau. Heute fällt es immer schwerer, die Stadtgrenze zu finden, aber der Durchmesser rückt allmählich an 100 Kilometer. Und ständig werden neue Bahnlinien gebaut – im vergangenen Jahr waren es zwei. Nichts deutet darauf hin, daß das Wachstum nachlassen könnte.

Die Bedingungen, mit denen sich der amerikanische Architekt Steven Holl bei seiner Wohnsiedlung Patios 11 in Makuhari auseinandersetzen mußte, erinnerten an sein »Stadtrand«-Projekt (»Edge of a City«) Ende der 80er Jahre. Da untersuchte er die Theorie, daß man, »um der wuchernden Ausbreitung im Randgebiet der Städte entgegenzuwirken, als vordringliches Ziel Räume und nicht Objekte schaffen« muß. Vier visionäre Städteplanungsprojekte für die Randgebiete von Dallas, Manhattan, Cleveland und Phoenix in den USA wurden dargelegt. Holl vertrat die Auffassung, daß die Schaffung »eines intensivierten städtischen Raumes als kohärenter Mittler zwischen den Extremen Metropole und Agrarbereich dienen könne«.

Als dieses Buch entstand, lag Patios 11

am Rande des Erschließungsgebiets; bald wird es jedoch von weiteren Wohnblocks eingeschlossen sein. Jeder Block wurde von einem anderen Architekten entworfen, um für Abwechslung zu sorgen, obwohl die Höhe von den Städteplanern festgelegt wurde und einheitliche Straßenfassaden vorgeschrieben sind. Zwar gibt es eine Reihe von interessanten Projekten, aber dennoch hat das Viertel etwas Erdrückendes. Obwohl sich die Gelegenheit geboten hatte, den Stadtrand neu zu überdenken, werden die Neuansätze wohl in den Schubladen der Planer verstauben.

Patios 11

Steven Holl Architects

1

2

3

1–3 The south courtyard house, 'House of Blue Shadow', is clad in brass panels. The adjacent main block is inflected to 'gently bend space'.

1–3 La maison sud de la cour, «La Maison de l'Ombre Bleue», est habillée de panneaux de cuivre. L'angle, légèrement incliné, du bloc adjacent façonne l'espace.

1–3 Das südliche Hofhaus, »Haus der blauen Schatten«, ist mit Messingblechen verkleidet. Der benachbarte Hauptblock soll mit seiner schrägen Fassade »den Raum sanft biegen«.

4–5 The east gatehouse, 'Sunlight Reflecting House', bridges the upper corners of two of the main blocks.

4–5 La loge est, «La Maison Miroir du Soleil», relie les angles de deux des blocs principaux.

4–5 Das östliche Pförtnerhaus, das »Sonnenlicht reflektierende Haus«, liegt an der oberen Ecke zweier Hauptblocks.

4

5

1

1 The south courtyard house seen
  from the west gate.
2 Opening beside the south
  courtyard house.

1 La loge sud, vue du portail ouest.
2 Ouverture à côté de la loge sud.

1 Das südliche Pförtnerhaus vom
  Westeingang aus gesehen.
2 Öffnung neben dem südlichen
  Pförtnerhaus.

2

1

1–2 The north courtyard house, 'Water
Reflecting House', is cantilevered
over a shallow pond.
3 Inside, light is reflected from
the surface of the water through
a glass wall and a glass panel in
the floor.

1–2 Loge nord, «La Maison Miroir
de l'Eau», est en porte-à-faux
au-dessus d'un plan d'eau peu
profond.
3 A l'intérieur, la lumière se réfléchit
de la surface de l'eau dans le
plancher par un mur de verre et un
panneau de verre dans le plancher.

1–2 Das nördliche Hofhaus, das
»Wasser reflektierende Haus«,
steht auf einem Ausleger über
einem flachen Teich.
3 Das Licht wird durch eine Glaswand und eine Glasplatte im Fußboden von der Wasseroberfläche in
den Innenraum reflektiert.

2

3

1–4 The rooftop north gatehouse is a circular structure surrounded by perforated aluminium panels.

1–4 Le toit de la loge nord est une structure ronde encerclée de panneaux d'aluminium perforé.

1–4 Das runde, nördliche Pförtnerhaus liegt hinter Aluminiumgittern in Dachhöhe.

4

1   2   3

1–8 The interiors of the six gatehouses
and courtyard houses are
characterised by their use of colour
and geometric openings. North
gatehouse (**1, 5**). East gatehouse (**2,
4, 6**). West gatehouse (**7**). South
courtyard house (**3, 8**).

1–8 L'intérieur des six loges et maisons
avec cour ont en commun
l'utilisation de couleurs et
d'ouvertures géométriques.
Loge nord (**1, 5**). Loge est (**2, 4, 6**).
Loge ouest (**7**). Maison avec cour
sud (**3, 8**).

1–8 Das Interieur der sechs Hof- und
Pförtnerhäuser wird durch den
Einsatz von Farben und geomet-
rischen Öffnungen gestaltet.
Nördliches Pförtnerhaus (**1, 5**).
Östliches Pförtnerhaus (**2, 4, 6**).
Westliches Pförtnerhaus (**7**).
Südliches Hofhaus (**3, 8**).

4   5

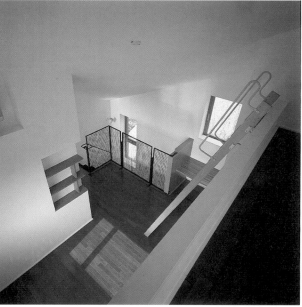

6   7

This residential project is composed primarily of four reinforced-concrete blocks stained yellow ochre, blue-grey and terracotta. These 'silent heavyweight buildings', their façades lightened by a rhythmic repetition of openings, define an urban space consisting of two inner courtyards and passageways to the apartments. The plans of the blocks are rectangular with slight inflections that 'gently bend space and passage, interrelating them with movement'.

The four blocks provide a backdrop for six smaller-scaled, individually designed gatehouses and courtyard houses – 'active lightweight structures'. In contrast to the functional minimalism of the blocks, these set out to celebrate natural phenomena:

the way the light changes in the course of the day, the views of the ocean and of distant Mount Fuji. These smaller structures are interspersed throughout the scheme and draw attention to its perspectival arrangement. Together they form a reference to a spiritual inner journey described in the Haiku of the fifteenth-century poet Matsuo Basho, 'The Narrow Road to the Deep North'. Each seems to have a parasitic dependency on a main 'heavyweight' body, emerging as rooftop growths, adjacent to an inner wall, set in a gap between two blocks, placed over a pond in an inner court.

The east gatehouse, 'Sunlight Reflecting House', is located at the upper corner of two blocks. Its angular form is clad with

aluminium panels and a protruding corner reflects sunlight down into the central courtyard. The circular north gatehouse, 'Colour Reflecting House', is situated at the opposite corner, surrounded by perforated aluminium panels. Sunlight is filtered through these panels to bounce off the vividly coloured exterior walls and is then reflected back into the windows as a diffused glow. The effect brightens and dims as the sun crosses the sky. The south gatehouse, 'House of Nothing', is a rooftop-level observation deck giving views of the ocean. A sculptural arrangement of beams panelled with copper forms a framework against the sky.

The north courtyard house, 'Water Reflecting House', serves as a communal

meeting room or tea-house. It is cantilevered over a shallow pond and light is reflected into the interior from the surface of the water through a glass wall and a glass panel in the floor. A skylight frames the sky. The south courtyard house, 'House of Blue Shadow', is also a public meeting room. It is clad with brass panels and small windows of various shapes introduce sunlight into the blue-plastered interior. The west gatehouse, 'House of Fallen Persimmon', is supported on nine stilts. Its slanting roof relates to the outward lean of the wall of the main block. This structure replaces an earlier design for a house 'dedicated to teleological suspension' that was to have been suspended on a frame between the

1

Ce projet de logements est principalement composé de quatre blocs en béton armé teintés en ocre, gris-bleu et brun. Ces «poids-lourds silencieux» et leurs façades allégées par répétition cadencée des ouvertures définissent un espace urbain qui est composé de deux cours intérieures et de passerelles menant aux appartements. Les plans des blocs sont rectangulaires avec de légères modulations qui «adoucissent légèrement l'espace et le passage, les reliant ainsi par le mouvement».

Les quatre immeubles offrent une toile de fond aux six loges et maisons avec cour – «les structures poids-plumes vivantes» conçues sur une plus petite échelle avec, pour chacune, un design différent. Elles contrastent avec le minimalisme

1 East elevation, southern end.
2 West elevation.
3 East elevation, northern end.

1 Elevation est, côté sud.
2 Elevation ouest.
3 Elevation est, côté nord.

1 Ostansicht, südliches Ende.
2 Westansicht.
3 Ostansicht, nördliches Ende.

Dieses Wohnobjekt besteht vorwiegend aus vier ockergelb, blau-grau und terra-kottafarben eingetönten Stahlbetonblocks. Diese »schweigenden, schwergewichtigen Gebäude«, deren Fassaden durch rhyth-misch wiederholte Öffnungen aufgelockert werden, definieren einen städtischen Raum aus zwei Innenhöfen und Passagen zu den Wohnungen. Der Grundriß der Blocks ist rechteckig mit leichten Beugungen, die »Raum und Gang leicht krümmen und sie zur Bewegung in Beziehung setzen«.

Die vier Blocks bilden den Hintergrund zu sechs individuell entworfenen Pförtner- und Hofhäusern – »aktive leichtgewichtige Strukturen«. Im Gegensatz zum funktio-nalen Minimalismus der Blocks sind diese so angelegt, daß sie Naturphänomene zele-

brieren: die Art, wie sich das Licht im Ver-laufe des Tages ändert, den Blick auf das Meer und den Fudschijama in der Ferne. Diese kleineren Strukturen sind über den Komplex verteilt und lenken die Aufmerk-samkeit auf dessen perspektivische Anord-nung. Gemeinsam stellen sie einen Bezug zu einer inneren, seelischen Reise her, wie sie im 15. Jahrhundert der Dichter Matsuo Basho in dem Haiku »Der schmale Weg in den hohen Norden« beschrieben hat. Jede dieser Strukturen befindet sich in scheinbar parasitärer Abhängigkeit von einem zen-tralen »Schwergewichts«-Körper; sie treten als Auswüchse auf dem Dach auf, neben einer Innenmauer, in der Lücke zwischen zwei Blocks, über einem Teich in einem der Innenhöfe.

Das östliche Pförtnerhaus, das »Son-nenlicht reflektierende Haus«, liegt an der oberen Ecke zweier Blocks. Seine kantige Form ist mit Aluminiumblechen ver-kleidet, und eine hervorstehende Ecke reflektiert das Sonnenlicht hinunter in den zentralen Innenhof. Das runde, nördliche Pförtnerhäuschen befindet sich an der gegenüberliegenden Ecke, umgeben von perforierten Aluminiumblechen. Das Son-nenlicht hat durch diese Paneele gefiltert, von den in leuchtenden Farben gehaltenen Außenmauern reflektiert und fällt dann nach nochmaliger Widerspiegelung als diffuses Leuchten auf die Fenster. Je nach der Sonnenstellung am Himmel wirkt der Effekt heller oder dunkler. Das südliche Pförtnerhäuschen, das »Haus des Nichts«,

main blocks. The final outcome is rather flat by comparison.

Light and intense colour interplay with solid and void. Holl's interest in Japanese architecture and in the work of artist James Turrell are well represented in this poetic scheme.

2

fonctionnel des blocs et sont là pour célébrer les phénomènes naturels: la variation de la lumière au cours de la journée, la vue sur l'océan et le Mont Fuji plus loin. Ces plus petites structures s'interposent sur tout le projet et mettent en valeur l'arrangement optique du lieu. Les deux structures sont une référence au haiku de Matsu Basho, un poète du 15ème siècle, intitulé «La route étroite vers le nord lointain» qui décrit un voyage spirituel intérieur. Chaque structure semble dépendre d'un corps «poids-lourd» principal et émerger comme des excroissances de toits, perpendiculaire à un mur intérieur, entre deux blocs ou au-dessus d'un plan d'eau dans une cour intérieure.

«La Maison Miroir du Soleil» est la loge est, située à l'angle de deux blocs. Sa forme angulaire est habillée de panneaux d'aluminium et un angle saillant réfléchit la lumière du soleil dans la cour centrale. La loge nord, «La Maison Miroir de la Couleur», est ronde et située à l'angle opposé, revêtue de panneaux d'aluminium perforés. La lumière du soleil passe par ces panneaux et se réfléchit sur les couleurs vives du mur extérieur, elle est ensuite renvoyée sur les fenêtres produisant une incandescence diffuse. L'effet augmente ou s'estompe selon le mouvement du soleil dans le ciel. «La Maison du Rien» est la tour d'observation au niveau du toit qui offre un point de vue sur l'océan. La disposition sculpturale des poutres

lambrissées de cuivre forme un encadrement dans le ciel.

«La Maison Miroir de l'Eau» est la maison avec cour, conçue comme une salle de réunion ou un salon de thé. Elle est en porte-à-faux au-dessus d'un plan d'eau peu profond. La lumière, qui se réfléchit dans la surface de l'eau, pénètre à l'intérieur par un mur de verre et un panneau de verre dans le sol. Une lucarne encadre le ciel. «La Maison de l'Ombre Bleue» est une maison avec cour, elle aussi conçue comme une salle de réunion. Elle est habillée de panneaux de cuivre et de petites fenêtres aux formes variées permettant à la lumière d'entrer dans l'intérieur couvert d'un enduit bleu. «La Maison du Kaki Tombé» est la loge ouest

portée par neuf pilotis. Son toit oblique rappelle l'inclinaison de l'angle du mur extérieur du bloc principal. En comparaison, le résultat final est un peu décevant.

La lumière et les couleurs vives jouent avec les pleins et les vides. L'intérêt de Holl pour l'architecture japonaise et pour le travail de l'artiste James Turrell ressortent bien dans cet aménagement poétique.

ist eine Aussichtsplattform auf Dachhöhe mit Ausblick aufs Meer. Eine skulpturähnliche Anordnung von kupfergetäfelten Balken ragt wie ein Rahmen in den Himmel.

Das nördliche Hofhaus, das »Wasser reflektierende Haus«, dient als Gemeindesaal oder Teehaus. Es steht auf einem Ausleger über einem flachen Teich, und das Licht wird durch eine Glaswand und eine Glasplatte im Fußboden von der Wasseroberfläche in den Innenraum reflektiert. Ein Dachfenster rahmt den Himmel ein. Das südliche Hofhaus, »Haus der blauen Schatten«, dient ebenfalls als Begegnungsstätte. Es ist mit Messingblechen verkleidet, und kleine Fenster von unterschiedlicher Form lassen Sonnenlicht in das blau verputzte Innere einfallen. Das

westliche Pförtnerhäuschen, »Haus der gefallenen Persimone«, steht auf neun Stelzen. Das Schrägdach stellt eine Beziehung zur Außenschräge der Hauptblockmauer dar. Diese Struktur ersetzt einen früheren Entwurf, der ein »der teleologischen Aufhängung gewidmetes« Haus darstellte; es sollte in einem Rahmen zwischen den Hauptblocks hängen. Im Vergleich dazu wirkt diese endgültige Lösung eher fade.

Licht und intensive Farben stehen im Wechselspiel mit Festkörpern und Leere. Holls Interesse an japanischer Architektur und an den Werken des Künstlers James Turrell kommt in diesem poetischen Projekt gut zum Ausdruck.

3

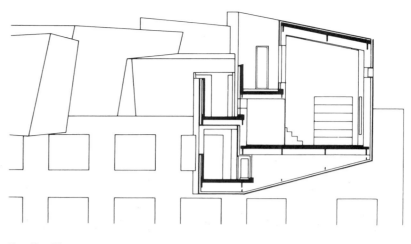

East Gate House
section A–A

Site plan

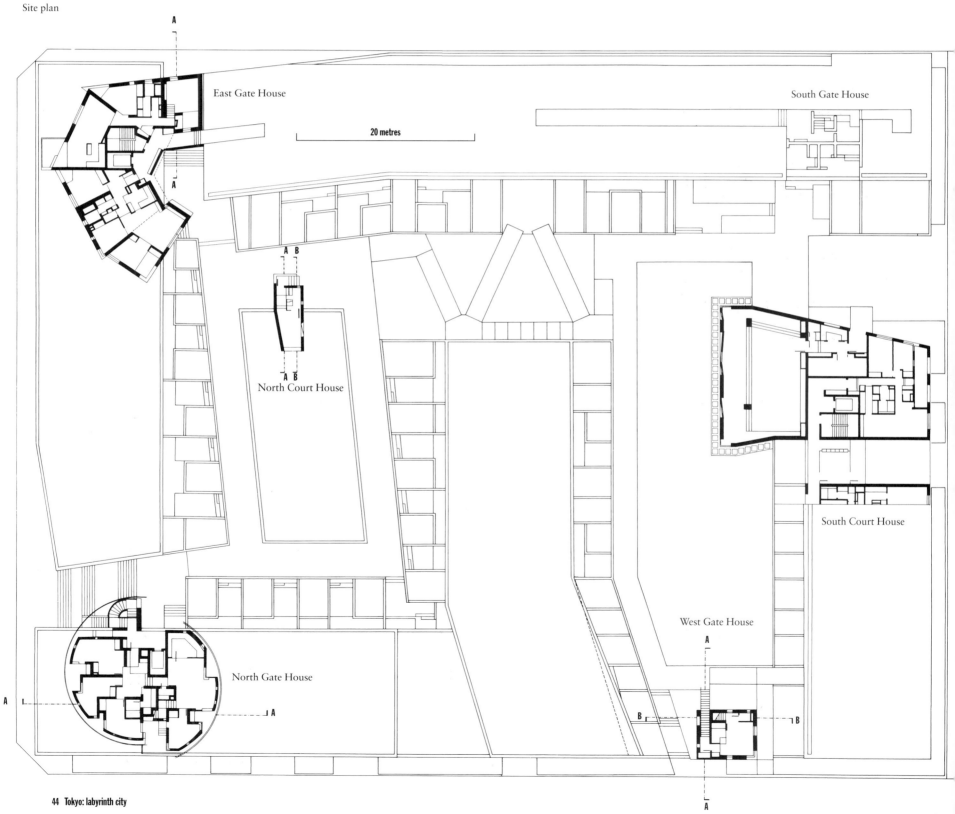

A

East Gate House

South Gate House

20 metres

A

A B

North Court House

A B

South Court House

West Gate House

A

North Gate House

B

B

A

A

A

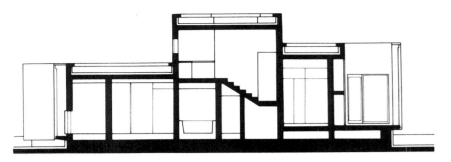

North Gate House
section A–A

Steven Holl Architects
Kouichi Sone + Environmental
Design Associates
Toshio Enomoto, Kajima Design
1996

Address 2-14 Uchise Mihama-ku, Chiba
Prefecture
Client Mitsui Fudosan Group
Contractor Kajima + Kaisei + Mitsui JV
Structural engineer Kajima Design/Keizo Miyagawa
Consultant Masaru Murata/Yosuke Taga
Landscape consultant JUKA Garden +
Architecture/Masato Kawashima
Lighting consultant L'Observatoire/Hervé Descotte
Design coordinator Kouichi Sone
Site area 8415 square metres
Size 26,944 square metres
Publications EL CROQUIS (2/96); GA JAPAN
(5/96); SHINKENCHIKU (5/96);
KENCHIKUBUNKA (6/96);

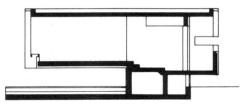

North Court House
section A–A

10 metres

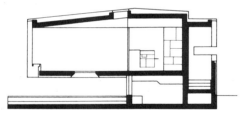

North Court House
section B–B

West Gate House
section A–A

West Gate House
section B–B

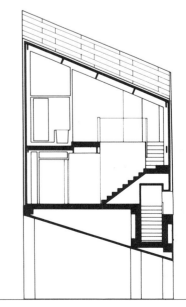

The 'unplanned', multifarious cityscape of Tokyo seems in vivid contrast to its highly stratified and orderly population. But despite its chaotic appearance, there is an underlying pattern to the city's structure.

Tokyo was originally made up of a series of rings spiralling outwards from a central castle. This totalitarian civic model is almost indiscernible today, buried under patch after patch of urban growth. The basis of this growth is by plots of land rather than by streets. Streets were largely allowed to take their own course, as long as they occupied as little space as possible. The fact that few of Tokyo's streets have names illustrates their secondary status. An extensive network of public thoroughfares linking areas and providing access is a relatively recent development that has been superimposed on the city plan without regard to the existing mass of plots and grids. The result is a layered sequence of fantastic complexity in which rigidity has given way to a flexible order. The cityscape grows organically, following the requirements of its millions of individuals.

Tokyo's streets rarely have a visual order. Wildly different building scales, functions and styles coexist, seeming to ignore each other. A myriad of individual aspirations and conditions are represented against the backdrop of elevated expressways and train lines. The effect is described by Donald Richie in A Lateral View (1991): 'Everywhere you look it is a chaos, but what a fascinating chaos it is. It is a mosaic city, a mélange city … There are hundreds of neighbourhoods in each district, and dozens of districts in each section, and tens of sections in this enormous city.'

The dialogue between the various parts of the city and its streets is the concern of Takeo Kimura of Tao Architects. For him, a building, like the fabric of the city, does not represent an integrated whole but rather is assembled from fragments of 'innumerable, various and diverse details which are never themselves unified'.

The form of Kimura's buildings evolves during the design process. He regards this process as the creation of a collage from various, sometimes opposed, concerns rather than the development of a unity of form and function as in modernism. The concerns to be taken into consideration include the demands of the client, legal restrictions, and the specifications of available mass-produced materials. The discrepancies between the requirements these elements make are not so much resolved as the differences revealed. While many designers feel they are struggling against the conflicts caused by the various factors to be taken into consideration, for Kimura these present an opportunity for design expression.

Kimura: 'I always think of multiple readings of the object when I design. Of course it can be read through its function alone, but it can also be read quite differently. But I always take the function as the most important factor because if an element doesn't have a clear function then the

Le paysage très varié et «inorganisé» de Tokyo apparaît comme un contraste extraordinaire par rapport à sa population hautement ordonnée et stratifiée. Mais de cette apparence chaotique émerge un agencement sous-jacent à la structure de la ville.

Tokyo est à l'origine constituée d'une séries d'anneaux formant une spirale vers l'extérieur du château central. Ce modèle administratif totalitaire n'est presque plus perceptible aujourd'hui, enfoui sous des morceaux et des morceaux de croissance urbaine. Cette croissance s'est opérée par lots de terrain et non pas par rues. On a très souvent laissé les rues suivre leur propre chemin pour autant qu'elles prenaient aussi peu de place que possible. Le fait que peu

Zwischen dem »planlosen«, abwechslungsreichen Stadtbild Tokios und der sozial vielschichtigen und ordnungsliebenden Bevölkerung scheint ein krasser Widerspruch zu herrschen. Aber trotz ihres chaotischen Erscheinungsbildes folgt die Struktur der Stadt einem Muster.

Tokio bestand ursprünglich aus einer Reihe von Ringen, die von einer zentralen Festung ausgehend spiralförmig nach außen verliefen. Dieses totalitäre Stadtmodell ist heute fast ganz verschwunden, begraben von einem Neubauflicken nach dem anderen. Dieses Wachstum erfolgt nach Grundstücken, nicht nach Straßenzügen. Die Straßen durften sich mehr oder weniger selbständig ihren Weg bahnen, vorausgesetzt, daß sie so wenig Platz wie möglich einnahmen. Daß nur wenige Straßen in Tokio einen Namen haben, unterstreicht ihre untergeordnete Bedeutung. Das umfassende Netz öffentlicher Durchgangsstraßen, die die verschiedenen Viertel miteinander verbinden und Zugang schaffen, entstand erst in jüngerer Zeit; es wurde dem Stadtplan ohne Rücksicht auf die bestehende Masse von Parzellen und Gittern aufgesetzt. Das Ergebnis ist eine Schichtenfolge von schier unglaublicher Komplexität, bei der Starrheit von flexibler Ordnung abgelöst wurde. Das Stadtbild verzeichnet ein organisches Wachstum, entsprechend den Bedürfnissen der Millionen von Einzelbewohnern.

Die Straßen Tokios folgen nur selten einem visuellen Ordnungsprinzip. Bauten, die in Maßstab, Funktion und Stil vollkommen voneinander abweichen, stehen nebeneinander, ohne sich gegenseitig Beachtung zu schenken. Eine Vielzahl individueller Erwartungen und Gegebenheiten zeichnet sich vor dem Hintergrund der Hochbahnen und Eisenbahnlinien ab. Die Wirkung wird von Donald Richie in A Lateral View (1991) folgendermaßen beschrieben: »Wohin man auch schaut, herrscht Chaos – aber wie faszinierend dieses Chaos doch ist. Es ist eine Mosaikstadt, eine Mélangestadt … in jedem Bezirk gibt es Hunderte von Vierteln, Dutzende von Bezirken in jedem Stadtteil, zig Stadtteile in dieser riesigen Stadt.«

Der Dialog zwischen den einzelnen Stadtteilen und ihren Straßen ist das Anliegen von Takeo Kimura von Tao Architects. Für ihn stellt ein Gebäude, ebenso wie die Bausubstanz der Stadt, nicht ein integriertes Ganzes

Fusions and subdivisions

multiplicity collapses from the base. It loses any significance. For instance, the sunblinds on Lars Bil are entirely functional, though they may be read as ships' masts, or something else.'

de rues aient un nom illustre aussi leur rôle secondaire. Le réseau étendu de voies publiques reliant les quartiers entre eux et permettant la circulation relève d'un aménagement relativement récent qui se superpose au plan de la ville sans tenir compte des lots et des quadrillages existants. Le résultat est un enchaînement par couches d'une complexité extraordinaire où la rigidité a cédé la place à un ordre souple. Le paysage de la ville se développe de façon organique selon les besoins de ses millions d'habitants.

Rares sont les rues qui ont un ordre apparent. Les échelles extrêmement variées des immeubles, les fonctions et les styles cohabitent tout en donnant l'impression de s'ignorer mutuellement. Une myriade de conditions et d'aspirations individuelles est

représentée avec en toile de fond des voies rapides aériennes et des lignes de chemins de fer. Donald Ritchie décrit ce paysage dans A Lateral View (1991): «Quel que soit l'endroit où les yeux se posent, c'est le chaos mais quel chaos fascinant! C'est une ville mosaïque, une ville de variété confuse [...]. On trouve des centaines de quartiers dans chaque arrondisement, une douzaine de arrondisement par secteur et des dizaines de secteur dans cette énorme ville».

Ce dialogue entre les différentes parties de la ville et de ses rues est le centre d'intérêt de Takeo Kimura de Tao Architects. Selon lui, un immeuble, à l'instar du tissu d'une ville, ne représente pas une entité intégrée mais plutôt un assemblage de fragments d' «innombrables détails

divers et variés qui ne forment jamais un tout».

La forme des immeubles de Kimura évolue au cours du processus de conception. Il considère ce processus comme la création d'un collage fait d'éléments variés et parfois opposés plutôt que le développement d'une unité de forme et la fonction, comme l'entend le mouvement moderne. Les éléments à prendre en considération sont les exigences du client, la législation et les caractéristiques des matériaux fabriqués en série. Les divergences quant aux conditions requises par ces matériaux ne sont pas forcément résolues au fur et à mesure qu'elles apparaissent. Alors que nombre de designers se débattent au milieu des problèmes causés par les divers facteurs à prendre en compte,

pour Kimura au contraire, ces facteurs sont une source potentielle d'inspiration à intégrer au design.

Kimura: «Quand je conçois quelque chose, je pense toujours aux multiples lectures de l'objet. On peut bien sûr le lire uniquement à travers sa fonction, mais on peut aussi le lire autrement. Cependant, je considère la fonction comme le facteur le plus important car si un élément n'a pas de fonction évidente, la multiplicité s'effondre à la base. Et l'objet perd tout son sens. Par exemple, les jalousies du bâtiment Lars Bil sont totalement fonctionnelles, pourtant elles peuvent se lire comme des mâts de bateau ou autre.»

dar, sondern setzt sich vielmehr aus Fragmenten »unzähliger unterschiedlicher und verschiedenartiger Details zusammen, die niemals zu einer Einheit verschmelzen«.

Die Form von Kimuras Gebäuden entwickelt sich im Laufe des Entwurfsprozesses. Er sieht diesen Vorgang als die Schaffung einer Collage aus unterschiedlichen, manchmal gegensätzlichen Anliegen – nicht als die Entwicklung einer Einheit von Form und Funktion wie beim Modernismus. Zu den Anliegen, die zu berücksichtigen sind, zählen die Wünsche des Kunden, gesetzliche Vorgaben sowie die Spezifikationen der verfügbaren, in Massenproduktion hergestellten Baumaterialien. Die durch die Anforderungen dieser Elemente entstehenden Diskrepanzen werden nicht beseitigt, sondern vielmehr aufgezeigt. Viele

Designer haben das Gefühl, gegen Konflikte ankämpfen zu müssen, die aus den vielen zu berücksichtigenden Faktoren erwachsen, aber Kimura sieht darin eine Gelegenheit zum entwerferischen Ausdruck.

Kimura: »Ich denke bei meinen Entwürfen immer an vielfältige Lesarten des Objekts. Man kann es natürlich ausschließlich funktional interpretieren, aber man kann es auch ganz anders sehen. Ich nehme allerdings die Funktion immer als wichtigsten Faktor, denn wenn ein Element keine klare Funktionalität besitzt, bricht die Vielfältigkeit schon an der Basis in sich zusammen. Sie verliert jede Bedeutung. Zum Beispiel sind die Markisen am Lars Bil rein funktional, obwohl man sie als Schiffsmasten oder irgend etwas anderes interpretieren kann.«

Lars Bil

Tao Architects

3

4

1–2 The basement is accessed from
wide, plaza-style steps.
3–5 An open inner courtyard has a fire
escape-style staircase that rises to
the entrance of the sixth-floor
residence.

1–2 L'accès au sous-sol se fait par de
grandes marches style esplanade.
3–5 L'escalier de la cour intérieure,
similaire à un escalier de secours,
s'élève jusqu'à l'entrée du logement
au sixième étage.

1–2 Das Souterrain erreicht man über
eine breite Treppe im Piazza-Stil.
3–5 Im offenen Innenhof erhebt sich
eine Art Feuertreppe bis zum
Eingang der Wohnung in der
sechsten Etage.

5

1

1–5 The staircase culminates at the
    uppermost two-storey apartment
    section, a smooth ovoid form clad
    in titanium-steel sheets.

1–5 L'escalier monte jusqu'à la partie
    supérieure dont la forme ovoïde
    bardée de feuilles en titane
    renferme la partie logement sur
    deux étages.

1–5 Die Treppe führt bis zum zwei-
    geschossigen Appartment ganz
    oben – eine glatter, eiförmiger
    Körper, mit Titanstahlblechen
    verkleidet.

2

— it replaces

3

4

5

1

2

1–3 Views around the inner courtyard.
  4 Front façade. The prefabricated
     factory-roofing material used to
     face the office section was too long
     for the required floor height and so
     had to be tilted outwards to fit.

1–3 Vues de la cour intérieure.
  4 Façade frontale. Le matériau
     préfabriqué pour toit d'usine,
     utilisé pour le revêtement de la
     partie bureau, s'est avéré plus long
     que la hauteur de sol requise et a
     dû être légèrement incliné vers
     l'extérieur pour s'intégrer.

1–3 Ansichten im Innenhof.
  4 Frontfassade. Die Verkleidungs-
     elemente des Büroteils – vorgefer-
     tigtes, gewelltes Hartglasmaterial,
     wie es normalerweise für Fabrik-
     dächer verwendet wird – paßten
     bei der vorgegebenen Etagenhöhe
     nur, indem sie nach außen gekippt
     wurden.

3

4

1–6 The protruding ovoid of the
uppermost residential part of the
building can be read as a ship's
hull (6), with the white steel frames
supporting the automatically
rolled sunblinds as ship's masts.

1–6 La forme ovoïde qui dépasse de
la partie supérieure et résidentielle
du bâtiment peut être lue comme
la coque d'un bateau (6), avec ses
ossatures en acier blanc portant
les brise-soleils qui s'enroulent
automatiquement, comme des
mâts de bâteau.

1–6 Die schimmernde Masse des
oberen Wohnbereichs ragt wie
ein Schiffsrumpf über die Straße
hinaus (6), während die wie
Masten wirkenden weißen Stahlrahmen zur Befestigung der
automatischen Markisen den
maritimen Eindruck verstärken.

1,3–6 The entrance hall is reached via a glazed bridge suspended over the basement (3). Inside is an extraordinary corrugated moulded column.
2 Dining room on the top floor.

1,3–6 L'accès au hall d'entrée se fait par un pont suspendu au-dessus du sous-sol (3). A l'intérieur, on trouve une extraordinaire colonne à la moulure ondulée.
2 Salle à manger au dernier étage.

1,3–6 Die Eingangshalle erreicht man über eine Glasbrücke, die über das Souterrain führt (3). Innen stößt man auf eine seltsam gewellte Säule.
2 Das Eßzimmer im Obergeschoß.

4

5

6

The Japan Railways' Yamanote loop surrounds the many subcentres that make up central Tokyo. The area in which this building is located is an interstice sandwiched between but belonging to none of the station-spawned subcentres of Shinjuku, Yotsuya, Iidabashi and Ikebukuro. The main street is characterised by a mismatch of differently scaled buildings sliced down and through to conform with successive sets of off-site light-control restrictions and limits on building heights. Two-storey housing, apartment blocks, small office buildings and other businesses are piled together. Half-hearted developments and cheap, tacked-on renovations are interspersed with traditional wooden buildings and gaping empty lots.

It is just this type of environment of disjunctive spaces and disparate styles, of fragmentary and scenic chaos, that provides the inspiration for Tao Architects. Lars Bil, an eight-storey assemblage of seemingly ad hoc industrial materials combined in a baroque manner, is located between a tiny traditional wooden shrine and a dull office block, opposite a glaring convenience store. The building is sited at one of the highest points of the city and has spectacular rooftop views.

Two different worlds are brought together. The upper part is a private residence with elements of a traditional town villa: sunny terraces, a secluded garden and large windows with sunshades. Below this are four floors of office space with a shop in the basement. An open inner courtyard with a staircase rises to the sixth floor. The two functions of the building are distinguished by the use of starkly contrasting materials and forms: 'a whole composed from fragments'.

This is the building of Mr Lar – 'Lars Bil' – who sailed to Japan from Taiwan. Two flats on the top two floors are occupied by his extended family and the fifth floor houses a further four flats that are rented out. Appropriately, the most striking element is an upper ovoid form covered in titanium-steel sheets – a 'ship's hull'. This suspended gleaming mass juts out slightly over the street. It is lodged into the roof of the villa-style fifth floor, which in turn is set atop an industrial-type concrete block. White steel frames protruding from the upper terrace support automatically rolled sunblinds. The office section is faced with prefabricated factory-roofing material in corrugated, reinforced glass and industrial floor grating is used for balustrades.

The main entrance hall is reached via a bridge suspended over the basement courtyard. Inside is an incompatible composition made up of a corrugated moulded column and a curved and polished red mortar wall which dissects the glass wall to the outside. The basement courtyard presents an equally surprising

La boucle du chemin de fer de Yamanote encercle la plupart des centres annexes qui forment le centre de Tokyo. Ce bâtiment se trouve dans un quartier étroit et comme pris en sandwich entre les centres annexes de Shinjuku, Yotsuya, Iidabashi et Ikebukuro qui se sont développés autour des gares locales existantes, sans toutefois se rattacher à l'un de ces centres. La rue principale est caractérisée par discordance de bâtiments d'échelles différentes qui ont été raccourcis et nivelés pour se conformer aux séries d'exigences de la législation sur le contrôle de l'altimétrie liée à l'ensoleillement et de la limitation des hauteurs d'immeuble. Les maisons de deux étages, immeubles de logements et petits immeubles de bureaux et autres sont coincés les uns contre les autres. Des aménagements bon marché et peu pensés ainsi que des rénovations superficielles côtoient des bâtiments traditionnels en bois et des parcelles non-construites.

C'est exactement ce type d'environnement, fait d'espaces sans unité aux styles disparates, de chaos fragmentaire et paysagé qui inspire Tao Architects. Lars Bil – un assemblage de huit étages fait de matériaux industriels qui semblent improvisés et agencés de façon baroque – est situé entre un petit bijou traditionnel en bois et un immeuble de bureaux sans intérêt et fait face à une épicerie éblouissante, et l'on a, du haut de l'immeuble, une vue spectaculaire.

Die Yamanote-Schleife der Japanischen Eisenbahn umläuft die vielen Teilbezirke, die das Herz Tokios bilden. Dieses Gebäude liegt im Niemandsland zwischen den durch Bahnhöfe ins Leben gerufenen Teilbezirken Shinjuku, Yotsuya, Iidabashi und Ikebukuro. An der Hauptstraße fallen vor allem die zusammengewürfelten Gebäude von unterschiedlicher Größe auf, die gestutzt und unterteilt worden sind, um diversen Bauvorschriften gerecht zu werden. Zweigeschossige Wohnhäuser, Wohnblocks, kleine Bürohäuser und andere gewerbliche Bauten stehen planlos nebeneinander. Halbherzige Neubauprojekte und billige Anbauten wechseln sich mit herkömmlichen Holzgebäuden und unbebauten Grundstücken ab.

Genau diese Art von Umgebung, mit unzusammenhängenden Räumen und widersprüchlichen Stilen, in der ein fragmentarisches und szenisches Chaos herrscht, liefert die Inspiration für Tao Architects. Lars Bil, eine achtstöckige Ansammlung von scheinbar ad hoc gewählten Industriematerialien, die auf barocke Weise miteinander kombiniert werden, liegt zwischen einem winzigen, traditionellen Holzschrein und einem langweiligen Bürohaus, gegenüber einem grellen Minimarkt. Das Gebäude steht auf einem der höchsten Punkte der Stadt, und vom Dach hat man eine spektakuläre Aussicht.

Zwei verschiedene Welten kommen hier zusammen. Der obere Teil ist eine Privatwohnung mit Elementen einer herkömmlichen Stadtvilla: sonnige Terrassen, ein abgeschiedener Garten und große Fenster mit Markisen. Darunter befinden sich vier Etagen mit Büroräumen sowie ein Geschäft im Souterrain. In einem offenen Innenhof steigt eine Treppe zur sechsten Etage auf. Die beiden Funktionen des Gebäudes werden durch die Verwendung kraß kontrastierender Materialien und Formen voneinander abgehoben: »Ein aus Fragmenten gebildetes Ganzes«.

Das ist das Gebäude des Herrn Lar – »Lars Bil« –, der mit dem Schiff von Taiwan nach Japan kam. Seine Großfamilie ist in zwei Wohnungen in den beiden oberen Geschossen untergebracht; in der fünften Etage befinden sich vier

sequence. Wide plaza-style steps lead down to a glass-walled space with porthole windows above.

The stepped-back and ovoid forms of the upper part of the building were the result of the requirements of off-site light-control restrictions. The prefabricated corrugated-glass panels covering the lower part were found to be slightly too long for the required floor height so they were fitted into place by tilting the panels outwards. This became an important stylistic feature. The resulting gap between glass and frame at the top is used as a ventilation system.

Deux univers différents sont réunis. La partie supérieure est un appartement privé fait à partir d'éléments du pavillon traditionnel: terrasse ensoleillée, jardin isolé et grandes fenêtres avec brise-soleil. La partie inférieures est constituée de quatre étages de bureaux avec un magasin en sous-sol. L'escalier de la cour intérieure ouverte s'élève jusqu'au sixième étage. Les deux fonctions de l'immeuble sont distinctes grâce aux formes et aux matériaux radicalement différents: «une entité composée de fragments».

C'est l'immeuble de Monsieur Lar – «Lars Bil» – qui navigua de Taiwan au Japon. Sa famille, très grande, occupe les deux appartements des deux étages supérieurs et les quatre appartements du

cinquième sont loués. Comme il se doit, l'élément le plus frappant est la forme ovoïde supérieure bardée de feuilles en titane – la «coque d'un bateau». Cette masse suspendue s'avance légèrement au-dessus de la rue. Elle est logée dans le toit du pavillon au cinquième étage, au-dessus duquel est placé un bloc de béton. Les structures en acier blanc qui dépassent de la terrasse supérieure maintiennent les brise-soleils qui s'enroulent automatiquement. La partie bureau est revêtue d'un matériau préfabriqué en verre renforcé et ondulé pour toit d'usine et, pour les balustrades, on a utilisé des grilles de plancher industriel.

On accède au hall principal par un pont suspendu au-dessus de la cour en

sous-sol. L'intérieur est une composition incompatible faite d'une colonne à la moulure ondulée et d'un mur courbe et poli en mortier rouge qui traverse le mur de verre vers l'extérieur. La cour en sous-sol offre un enchaînement tout aussi surprenant. Les grandes marches style esplanade descendent vers l'espace aux parois en verre, surmontées de fenêtres-hublots.

Les formes ovoïdes et en retrait de la partie supérieure de l'immeuble répondent aux exigences imposées par la législation en matière d'altimétrie par rapport à l'ensoleillement. Les panneaux préfabriqués de verre ondulé se sont révélés être légèrement trop longs par rapport à la hauteur d'étage autorisée et

ont dû être courbés vers l'extérieur de façon à pouvoir être installés. Cet aspect est devenu une caractéristique stylistique majeure de l'immeuble. Le vide laissé entre le verre et la structure supérieure est utilisé comme système de ventilation.

Mietwohnungen. Treffenderweise ist das auffälligste Element ein eiförmiger, mit Titanstahlblechen verkleideter Körper im oberen Teil – ein »Schiffsrumpf«. Diese schimmernde Masse ragt etwas über die Straße hinaus. Sie ist im Dach der im Villa-stil gehaltenen fünften Etage verankert, die ihrerseits auf einem industriell wirkenden Zementblock sitzt. Von der oberen Terrasse treten weiße Stahlrahmen hervor, an denen Markisen mit Aufrollautomatik hängen. Der Büroteil ist mit vorgefertigtem, gewelltem Hartglasmaterial verkleidet, das normalerweise für Fabrikdächer verwendet wird, und industrielle Fußbodenroste dienen als Balustraden.

Die Haupteingangshalle erreicht man über eine Brücke, die über den Innenhof

des Souterrains führt. In der Halle befindet sich eine Komposition aus Elementen, die gar nicht zusammenpassen wollen: eine gewellte, geformte Säule und eine gebogene, polierte, rot verputzte Wand, die die Glaswand nach außen unterteilt. Der Hof des Souterrains bietet eine ähnlich überraschende Abfolge. Eine breite Treppe im Piazza-Stil führt in einen von Glaswänden eingefaßten Raum, auf den Bullaugenfenster herabschauen.

Die gestuften und eiförmigen Körper des oberen Gebäudeteils waren das Ergebnis der Bauvorschriften. Es stellte sich heraus, daß die vorgefertigten Wellglasplatten, mit denen der untere Teil verkleidet ist, für die vorgeschriebene Etagenhöhe etwas zu lang waren, daher

neigte man die Platten beim Montieren nach außen. Daraus wurde ein wichtiges Stilmerkmal. Der resultierende Spalt zwischen Glas und Rahmen an der Oberseite dient als Belüftungssystem.

10 metres

Site plan

Ground floor plan

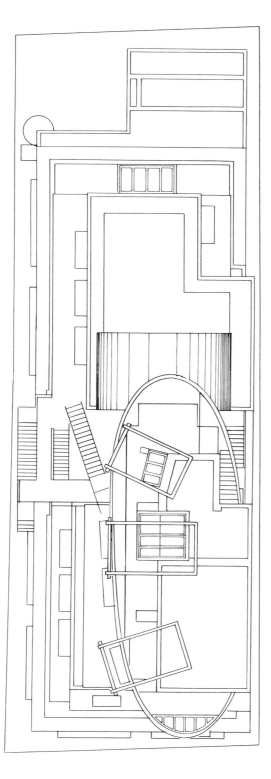

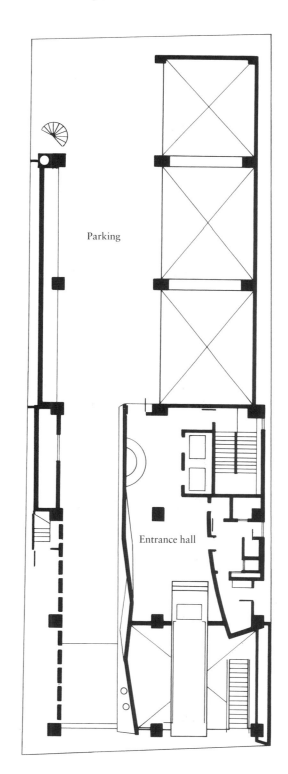

Parking

Entrance hall

Tao Architects
1994
Address Shinjuku-ku, Tokyo
Client Mr Lar
Contractor Goyo Construction
Structural engineer Ikeda Sekkei, Ltd
Site area 687 square metres`
Size 2949 square metres
Publications NIKKEI ARCHITECTURE (no 500)

First floor plan

Sixth floor plan

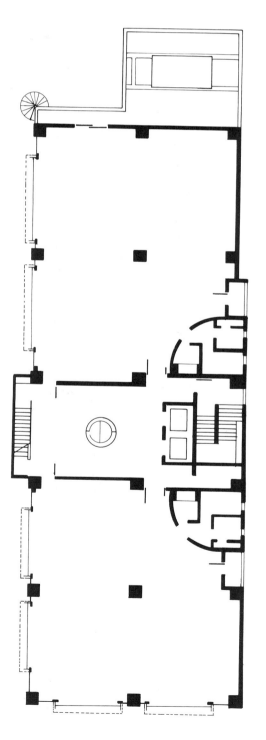

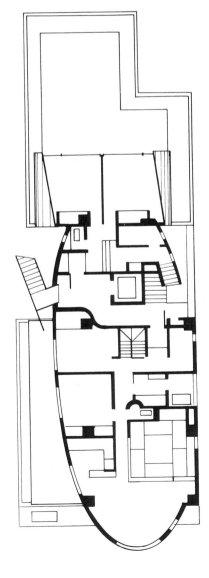

In 1960 Kenzo Tange published a radical urban plan for Tokyo. Its extraordinary scope and innovation made waves in architectural and planning departments around the world. A 30-kilometre-long bridge with adjoining piers was to cut across Tokyo Bay connecting the bayside business centre and Chiba district. Office space, schools and public facilities were arranged in elevated units suspended like beams between post-like core structures. Housing was located beneath vast sloping roofs that recalled traditional farmhouses. The mighty central axis was overlaid with a system of uncompromisingly straight highways and monorails to solve the problems of city congestion. Although its feasibility was questionable, the plan was a stroke of astounding boldness.

One scans Tange's FCG headquarters building, which stands in the vicinity of his 1960 plan, for traces of his earlier vision.

The role of the 'land standard' in Japan's economy is analogous to that of the gold standard in the economies of the world. While Japan may seem to be plugged into the twentieth-century global economic system, this is belied by the enormous value placed on land. The Shinto ceremony jichinsai, which is held on plots of land before construction begins, testifies to the sacred significance of land as well as to its economic value. Leafy bamboo fronds are planted at the corners of an earthen mound, around which is strung a rope to mark out a sacred enclosure.

Investment in land in Japan's cities was considered to be without risk, so ownership of land acted as a fail-safe collateral to raise funds for other ventures. This mentality was largely responsible for the spiralling price of land during the 1980s which underwrote the 'bubble' economy that flourished during that decade. Then the unthinkable happened and the market collapsed. The financial vacuum that resulted continues to slow the pace of economic recovery.

'The modern skyline of Tokyo is not beautiful, but it is a pretty faithful reflection of the realities of power,' writes Peter Popham in Tokyo, The City at the End of the World (1985). 'It's dynamic, too; it never stops changing. And in its endless, anarchic shifting and shaking down, it sometimes captures some aspect of the process of change with a fidelity hard to match with mere words.'

Popham suggests that with the right combination of money, ambition, connections and fixable restrictions, the creation of buildings as highly desirable badges of power is virtually unstoppable.

The city exposition 'Tokyo Frontier', which was due to open in March 1996 and run for 200 days, has been ignominiously cancelled. An international array of companies and organisations, as well as 20 million visitors, were expected to attend and the show was to provide a dramatic opening for the 448-hectare development Rinkai Fukutoshin (the Tokyo Metropolitan Waterfront subcentre). With Kenzo Tange at the helm of the organising committee, the event was expected to repeat the success of similar expositions held at Kobe and Yokohama.

Kenzo Tange publia en 1960 un plan d'urbanisme radicalement nouveau dont l'ambition et l'innovation extraordinaires ont eu un impact sur les architectes et les urbanistes du monde entier. Un pont d'une longueur de 30 kilomètres avec des môles attenants traverserait la Baie de Tokyo pour relier le centre d'affaires du front de mer et le quartier de Chiba. Bureaux, écoles et équipements publics seraient agencés en unités surélevées, suspendues comme des poutres entre les noyaux-poteaux des ossatures. L'habitation serait chapeautée d'immenses toits en pentes rappelant les fermes traditionnelles. L'imposant axe central serait surmonté d'un système rigide d'autoroutes et de monorails rectilignes afin d'éviter tout problème d'encombrement en ville. Même si la faisabilité du projet était discutable, il faisait, à n'en pas douter preuve d'une audace extraordinaire.

Passons en revue l'immeuble FCG de Tange à la recherche de traces de ses conceptions antérieures.

Le rôle de «l'étalon-terre» dans l'économie japonaise est analogue à celui de l'étalon-or dans les économies mondiales. Le Japon semble être au coeur du système économique mondial du vingtième siècle, mais cela est contredit par la valeur colossale de la terre. Le rituel de la cérémonie Jichinsai qui se tient sur un chantier avant le début de la construction est la preuve du sens sacré de la terre ainsi que de sa valeur. On plante des frondes de bambou feuillu au coin d'un tas de terre

Im Jahre 1960 veröffentlichte Kenzo Tange einen radikalen Städtebauplan für Tokio. So weitgefaßt und innovativ war dieser Plan, daß er in Architekturbüros und Planungsabteilungen überall auf der Welt Wellen schlug. Eine 30 Kilometer lange Brücke mit Piers sollte über die Bucht von Tokio geschlagen werden und das an der Bucht liegende Geschäftszentrum mit dem Chiba-Viertel verbinden. Büroräume, Schulen und öffentliche Einrichtungen waren in Hängekomplexen untergebracht, die wie Balken zwischen säulenähnlichen Kernstrukturen befestigt waren. Die Wohnkomplexe waren durch riesige, schräge Dächer geschützt, die an traditionelle Bauernhäuser erinnerten. Auf der mächtigen Mittelachse ruhten kompromißlos schnurgerade Autobahnen und Ein-schienenbahnen, die die Probleme des Verkehrsgedränges in der Stadt lösen sollten. Obwohl die Durchführbarkeit als fraglich gelten mußte, besaß der Plan ganz ohne Zweifel eine erstaunliche Kühnheit.

Man sucht Tanges FCG-Gebäude, unweit vom Schauplatz seines Planes von 1960, nach Spuren seiner damaligen, verwegenen Vision ab.

Die Rolle des »Landstandards« in der japanischen Wirtschaft ist der des Goldstandards in anderen Wirtschaftssystemen der Welt vergleichbar. Während es so schei-nen mag, als sei Japan mit Überzeugung am globalen Wirtschaftssystem des 20. Jahr-hunderts beteiligt, spricht der ungeheuer große Wert, der dem Land beigemessen wird, dagegen. Die Shinto-Zeremonie Jichinsai, die vor Baubeginn auf einem Grundstück abgehalten wird, unterstreicht nicht nur den finanziellen Wert des Landes, sondern auch seine religiöse Bedeutung. Belaubte Bambuswedel werden an den Ecken eines aufgeschütteten Erdhaufens eingepflanzt; daran wird ein Seil aufgehängt, und das so umfriedete Stück Land gilt als heilig.

In japanischen Städten in Land zu investieren galt als risikolos; das heißt, Landbesitz galt als hundertprozentig verbürgte Sicherheit, über die man andere Projekte finanzieren konnte. Diese Mentalität war weitgehend für den scharfen Anstieg der Grundstückspreise in den 80er Jahren verantwortlich, die ihrerseits die Grundlage der »Konjunkturblase« jener Zeit bildete. Dann geschah das Undenkbare, und der Markt

It was also to provide a glorious swansong for governor of Tokyo Shun-ichi Suzuki. However, enthusiasm for the event dwindled in the post-bubble era, and in 1995 Yukio Aoshima, a popular television comedian, won the election for governor of Tokyo with a promise to cancel the exhibition and thereby stop wasting taxpayers' money. The final joke came when it was realised that it would take an equal amount of public funds to pay the compensation demanded by the companies involved.

The skyline: badges of power

autour duquel on tend une corde pour marquer une enceinte sacrée.

L'investissement terrien dans les villes japonaises était considéré comme une valeur refuge et la propriété de terres servait de sûreté intégrée parallèle permettant de réunir des fonds pour créer d'autres entreprises. Ce mode de pensée est en grande partie responsable de l'inflation des prix du terrain pendant les années 80 qui a permis à l'économie «bubble» de prospérer durant cette décennie. L'impensable s'est produit et le marché s'est effondré. Le vide financier qui s'en est suivi continue de freiner la reprise économique.

«La ligne d'horizon du Tokyo d'aujourd'hui n'est pas belle mais elle est fidèle à l'image des réalités du pouvoir» constate Peter

Popham dans Tokyo, the city at the end of the world (1985). «Elle est aussi pleine d'énergie et ne cesse jamais de changer. Et si elle change sans cesse, traversant des périodes anarchiques, il lui arrive aussi de capter une partie de ce processus de changement avec une fidélité difficile à traduire avec de simples mots.» Pour Popham, tant que l'on saura habilement combiner l'argent, l'ambition, les relations et contourner la législation, il sera pratiquement impossible de freiner la construction d'immeubles qui sont les emblèmes d'une puissance très convoitée.

L'exposition «La frontière de Tokyo», qui devait s'ouvrir en mars 1996 pour une durée de six mois, a été honteusement annulée. Un nombre impressionnant de sociétés et d'organisations internationales ainsi que 20

millions de visiteurs étaient attendus et l'exposition aurait été l'occasion d'inaugurer en grande pompe l'aménagement de Rinkai Fukotoshin réalisé sur une surface de 448 hectares (centre annexe du Front de Mer de la Mégapole de Tokyo). Avec Kenzo Tange, comme président du comité d'organisation, l'événement aurait dû remporter un succès analogue à celui des expositions similaires à Kobe et Yokohama. Et cela aurait été l'occasion pour pour Shun-ichi Suzuki, le gouverneur de la ville de Tokyo de «chanter un glorieux chant du cygne». Mais, l'ère du «bubble» étant révolue, l'enthousiasme pour cet événement est peu à peu retombé. Puis, en 1995 Yukio Aoshima, le célèbre comique de télévision, a remporté les élections municipales de Tokyo en

promettant d'annuler l'exposition afin d'arrêter le gaspillage de l'argent des contribuables. Le clou de l'histoire est que le dédommagement des sociétés participantes coûtera autant que le budget public prévu pour ce projet.

brach zusammen. Das daraus resultierende finanzielle Vakuum drosselt noch immer das Tempo des wirtschaftlichen Wiederaufschwungs.

»Die moderne Skyline von Tokio ist nicht schön, aber sie spiegelt die Realitäten der Macht ziemlich genau wider«, schreibt Peter Popham in Tokyo, the city at the end of the world (Tokio, die Stadt am Ende der Welt – 1985). »Sie ist auch dynamisch – sie ändert sich ständig. Und durch dieses endlose, anarchische Sich-Verschieben und Sich-Einspielen fängt sie manchmal einen Aspekt des Wandlungsprozesses so wahrheitsgetreu ein, daß man mit bloßen Worten kaum nachkommen kann.« Wenn die richtige Kombination von Geld, Ehrgeiz, Beziehungen und umgehbaren Einschränkungen vorliegt, meint Popham, läßt

sich kaum verhindern, daß Gebäude als höchst reizvolle Symbole der Macht errichtet werden.

Die Ausstellung »Tokyo Frontier«, die im März 1996 eröffnet werden und 200 Tage laufen sollte, wurde unter beschämenden Umständen abgesagt. Eine Vielzahl von internationalen Unternehmen und Organisationen sowie 20 Millionen Besucher wurden erwartet; die Ausstellung sollte der dramatische Auftakt zur Eröffnung des 448 Hektar umfassenden Bauprojekts Rinkai Fukutoshin (im Teilbezirk Tokio-Hafen) sein. Man erwartete, daß die Veranstaltung, mit Kenzo Tange als Leiter des Organisationskomitees, ähnlich erfolgreich sein würde wie vergleichbare Ausstellungen in Kobe und Yokohama. Sie sollte auch einen ruhmreichen Schwanen-

gesang für den Gouverneur von Tokio, Shun-ichi Suzuki, darstellen. Doch nachdem die Konjunkturblase geplatzt war, schwand die Begeisterung für die Veranstaltung. 1995 gewann der beliebte Fernsehkomiker Yukio Aoshima die Wahl zum Gouverneur von Tokio mit dem Versprechen, die Ausstellung abzusagen und damit der Verschwendung von Steuergeldern Einhalt zu gebieten. Der Witz an der ganzen Sache war, daß man zur Zahlung des von den betroffenen Unternehmen geforderten Schadenersatzes eine ähnlich hohe Summe an öffentlichen Geldern aufbringen mußte.

FCG headquarters

Kenzo Tange Associates

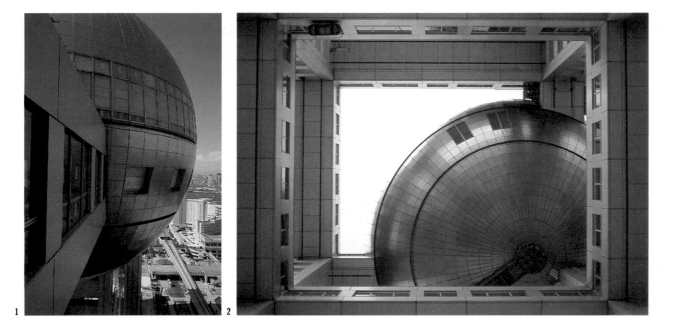

1

2

1–4 The two towers housing offices
and studios are connected by a
framework of 'corridors in the sky'
that supports a 32-metre-diameter
sphere containing a viewing port
and restaurant.

1–4 Les deux tours renfermant les
bureaux et les studios sont reliées
par une ossature faite de «couloirs
dans le ciel» qui soutient une
sphère de 32 mètres de diamètre
contenant un restaurant et une
plate-forme d'observation.

1–4 Die beiden Büro- und Studiotürme
werden durch ein Gerüst aus
»Himmelsgängen« miteinander
verbunden, auf dem eine 32 m
große Aussichtskugel mit Restaurant ruht.

3

4

1

2

1–4 The superstructure is clad in aluminium with dark-blue glass panels and clear glazing infil. The intention is to reveal the 24-hour operation of the building from the outside.

1–4 La superstructure est revêtue d'aluminium, de panneaux de verre bleu-foncé et de verre de remplissage transparent. L'effet recherché est de faire voir que cet immeuble fonctionne 24 heures sur 24.

1–4 Die Verkleidung des Oberbaus besteht aus Aluminium mit dunkelblauen Glasplatten und klaren Glaseinsätzen. Dadurch soll bereits von außen der 24-stündige Betrieb im Gebäude sichtbar sein.

3

4

1

2

3

1–3 A grand open staircase, still under construction, will give access to a 'hanging garden' on the roof of the base section.
4 Bayside façade.

1–3 Le majestueux escalier, une fois fini, permettra d'accéder au jardin suspendu au-dessus du toit de base entre les deux tours.
4 Façade en front de mer.

1–3 Eine große, offene Treppe, die sich noch im Bau befindet, wird einmal zu dem »hängenden Garten« über dem Sockel führen.
4 Fassade zur Bucht.

Take the driverless Yurikamome line from JR Shinbashi out towards Rinkai Fukutoshin, the new development built on reclaimed land in Tokyo Bay. The line runs alongside the bayside wharves and below the elevated expressway. As the train ascends above the roofline of the buildings, the spectacular Rainbow Bridge comes into view. Standing behind this on the farther shore is Kenzo Tange's latest addition to the Tokyo skyline, the new headquarters of the Fuji-Sankei Communications Group. The building houses Fuji Television and Nippon Broadcasting, and the proportions of the 25-storey structure replicate those of the new wide-screen, hi-vision television sets. As the train line loops up to join the

bridge, the massive scale of the building – 210 metres long and 120 metres high – becomes apparent.

Two towers are set on a seven-storey base. The western tower contains mainly offices while the other provides space for studios. Parking, a theatre, larger studios and related facilities are located in the base. The towers are connected by a framework of 'corridors in the sky' which supports a 32-metre-diameter sphere. The 'super *ramen* structure' is made visible across the façade, contributing to a unified design expression. The sphere is panelled with titanium and the main frame is covered in aluminium cladding with dark-blue glass panels and clear glazing infil. The central elevator shaft and other

features are predominantly glazed. The intention is to reveal from the outside the continuous 24-hour operation of the building. The flow of information and a multimedia network for the future are represented on the façade.

Though this is a private building, public access was an important consideration in the design. The extensive 'corridors in the sky' serve mainly as viewing walkways and the sphere contains a viewing port as well as a restaurant. The roof of the base section will be a 'hanging garden' with dramatic views of the framework above and across the bay. This area can be reached by ascending a grand open staircase that runs the length of the eastern tower. At the foot of this is an open plaza

which in the future may be used to stage events that can be watched from the steps.

In 1990, when the government unveiled its plan for the Tokyo Metropolitan Waterfront subcentre, 394 companies rushed to apply for building rights for the 18 available plots of land. In the present climate of confusion and uncertainty following the collapse of the economic bubble, many companies have pulled out, and the new train line winds its way past only those schemes that have survived the turmoil.

Today, if you stand at the centre of the 'hanging garden' and turn away from the bay, you see vast tracts of seemingly abandoned land stretching away into the distance.

1

Prenez la ligne automatique de Yurikamome qui part de la gare JR Shinbashi vers le Rinkai Fukutoshin, le nouvel aménagement construit sur un terrain pris sur mer dans la Baie de Tokyo. La ligne longe les quais de la baie et passe sous la voie rapide aérienne. Alors que le train s'élève au dessus de la ligne des toits, on voit apparaître le spectaculaire pont Arc-en-ciel. Derrière, plus loin sur le rivage, se dresse la dernière contribution à la ligne d'horizon de Tokyo de Kenzo Tange. C'est le nouveau siège social du groupe Fuji-Sankei Communication. L'immeuble abrite les chaînes de Fuji Television et Nippon Broadcasting et les proportions de cette structure de 25 étages reflètent celles des postes de

1 The massively scaled building towers above the surrounding reclaimed land.
2–3 The 'corridors in the sky' and offices give views of other parts of the structure and across the bay.

1 Les tours d'une échelle démesurée sur le terrain pris sur mer.
2–3 Les «couloirs dans le ciel» et les bureaux donnent sur d'autres éléments de la structure ainsi que de la baie de l'autre côté.

1 Die Türme des mächtig konzipierten Gebäudes erheben sich beherrschend über dem Erschließungsareal.
2–3 Die »Himmelsgänge« und Büros eröffnen den Blick auf andere Teile des Gebäudes und über die Bucht.

Man fährt mit der Yurikamome-Linie – die ohne Fahrer verkehrt – von JR Shinbashi in Richtung Rinkai Fukutoshin – einem Neubaukomplex, der auf neu gewonnenem Land in der Bucht von Tokio entstanden ist. Die Strecke streift die Kais, die die Bucht säumen, verläuft aber unterhalb der Expreß-Hochbahn. Wo die Bahn über das Dachniveau der Gebäude aufsteigt, kommt die spektakuläre Regenbogen-Brücke ins Blickfeld. Dahinter ragt am gegenüberliegenden Ufer Kenzo Tanges neuester Beitrag zur Skyline Tokios empor: der neue Hauptsitz der Fuji-Sankei Communication Group. In dem Gebäude sind die Fernsehgesellschaften Fuji Television und Nippon Broadcasting untergebracht, und das 25-stöckige Bauwerk hat die

gleichen Proportionen wie die neuen Breitwand-Hi-Vision-Fernsehgeräte. In dem Moment, wo die Bahn eine Schleife fährt, um auf die Brücke zu gelangen, erkennt man die Wucht des 210 m langen und 120 m hohen Gebäudes.

Zwei Türme sitzen auf einem siebenstöckigen Sockel. Im Westturm sind vor allem Büros untergebracht, während sich im anderen Turm Studios befinden. Im Sockel befinden sich Parkplätze, ein Theater, die größeren Studios und damit verbundene Einrichtungen. Die Türme werden durch ein Gerüst aus »Himmelsgängen« miteinander verbunden, auf dem eine Kugel von 32 m Durchmesser ruht. Die »Super-Ramen-Struktur« ist über die gesamte Breite der Fassade sichtbar, was

zu einem einheitlichen Designausdruck beiträgt. Die Kugel ist mit Titaniumblechen verkleidet; die Verkleidung des Hauptgerüsts besteht aus Aluminium mit dunkelblauen Glasplatten und klaren Glaseinsätzen. Der Hauptaufzugschacht und andere Baukörper sind weitgehend verglast. Dahinter verbirgt sich der Wunsch, bereits von außen den 24-stündigen Betrieb im Gebäude sichtbar werden zu lassen. Die Fassade bildet den Informationsfluß und ein Multimedianetz der Zukunft ab.

Obwohl es sich nicht um ein öffentliches Gebäude handelt, spielte der Zugang für die Öffentlichkeit eine wichtige Rolle bei dem Entwurf. Die weitläufigen »Himmelsgänge« dienen vor allem als Fußwege

2

télévision avec écran audio-panoramique. Tandis que le train fait une boucle pour rejoindre le pont, on découvre la taille impressionnante du bâtiment: 210 mètres de long sur 120 mètres de haut.

Les deux tours reposent sur une base de sept étages. La tour ouest est réservée aux bureaux, l'autre aux studios. Le parking, le théâtre, de plus grands studios et autres équipements sont situés dans la base. Les tours sont reliées par une ossature faite de «couloirs dans le ciel» qui soutient une sphère de 32 mètres de diamètre. A travers la façade on peut voir la «super structure à ossature» qui donne une cohérence à la conception de l'ensemble. La sphère est bardée de panneaux de titane et l'ossature principale est revêtue d'aluminium, de panneaux de verre bleu-foncé et de verre de remplissage transparent. La cage de l'ascenseur central et d'autres éléments sont réalisés principalement en verre. L'effet recherché est de faire voir que cet immeuble fonctionne 24 heures sur 24. Sur la façade apparaissent des informations en continu et un réseau multimédia du futur.

Bien que ce soit un immeuble privé, l'accès au public était un élément important de la conception. Les immenses «couloirs dans le ciel» jouent essentiellement un rôle de passerelle d'observation tout comme la sphère qui contient aussi un restaurant avec une plate-forme d'observation. Le toit de la base sera un «jardin suspendu» avec une vue spectaculaire sur l'ossature suspendue au-dessus et tout le front de mer. On accède à cet espace en prenant le majestueux escalier ouvert qui court le long de la tour est. Au pied de cette dernière se déroule une esplanade où pourront avoir lieu des spectacles qui se regarderont assis sur les marches.

Quand le gouvernement a dévoilé en 1990 le centre annexe du Front de Mer de la Mégapole de Tokyo, 394 sociétés se sont précipitées pour obtenir leur candidature pour un permis de construire sur les 18 lots de terrain disponibles. Étant donné le climat de confusion et d'incertitude qui règne depuis la chute du «bubble» économique, un grand nombre de ces sociétés se sont désistées et la nouvelle ligne de train serpente le long des quelques réalisations qui ont survécu à la tempête.

Aujourd'hui, si vous vous tenez au centre du «jardin suspendu», le dos tourné à la baie, vous voyez sous vos yeux d'immenses étendues de terrain qui semblent abandonnées et qui s'étendent à perte de vue.

für Besichtigungszwecke, und die Kugel beherbergt nicht nur ein Aussichtsfenster, sondern auch ein Restaurant. Der Sockel soll von einem »hängenden Garten« überdacht werden, von dem aus man einen eindrucksvollen Blick auf das darüber aufragende Gerüst und hinaus auf die Bucht haben wird. In diesen Teil gelangt man über eine große, offene Treppe, die über die gesamte Länge des Ostturms verläuft. Am Fuße des Turms liegt ein offener Platz, der in Zukunft für Veranstaltungen genutzt werden könnte; Zuschauer könnten auf der Treppe Platz finden.

Im Jahre 1990, als die Regierung ihren Plan für den Teilbezirk Tokio-Hafen bekanntgab, bewarben sich über Nacht 394 Unternehmen um Baugenehmigungen für die 18 verfügbaren Grundstücke. Im gegenwärtig verstörten Klima nach dem Platzen der Konjunkturblase haben viele dieser Unternehmen einen Rückzieher gemacht, und die neue Bahnlinie kurvt nur um die Projekte herum, die die Turbulenzen unbeschadet überstanden haben.

Steht man heute inmitten des »hängenden Gartens« und wendet sich von der Bucht ab, erstreckt sich ein riesiges, scheinbar verlassenes Areal bis in die Ferne.

3

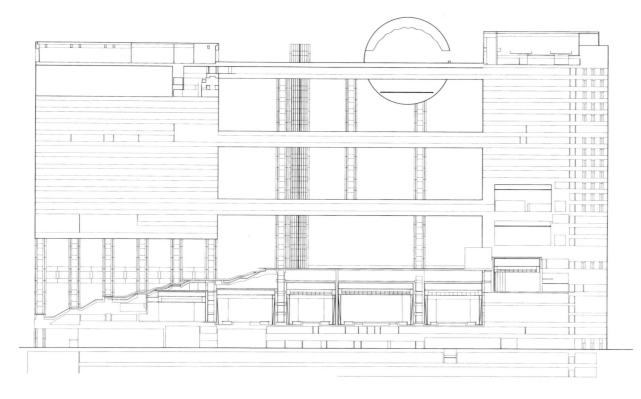

100 metres

Long section

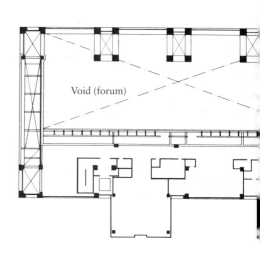

Void (forum)

Twenty-fourth floor plan

50 metres

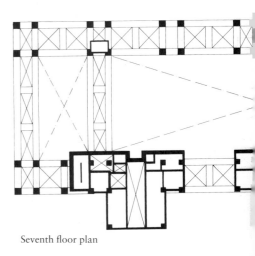

Seventh floor plan

Kenzo Tange Associates
1996
Address 2-4-8 Daiba Minato-ku, Tokyo
Client Fuji Television
Contractor Kajima Corporation
Structural engineer Kobori Research Complex, Inc.
Site area 21,102 square metres
Size 142,789 square metres

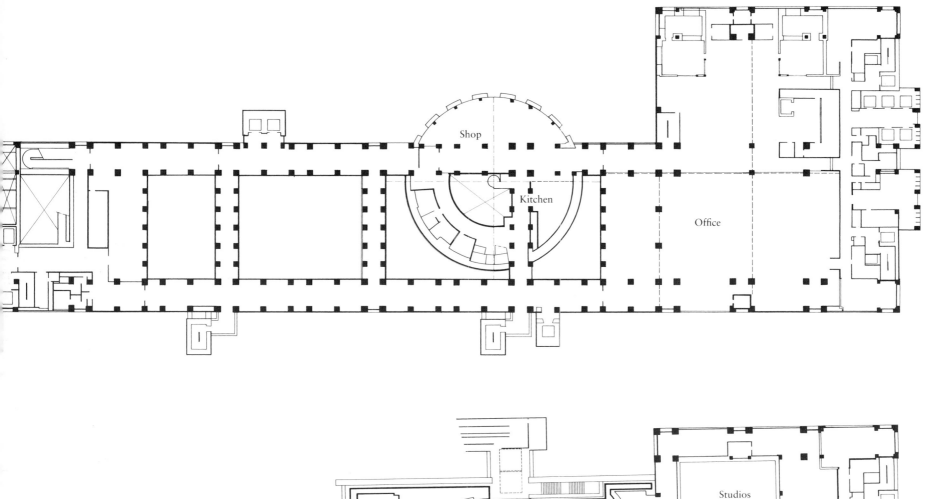

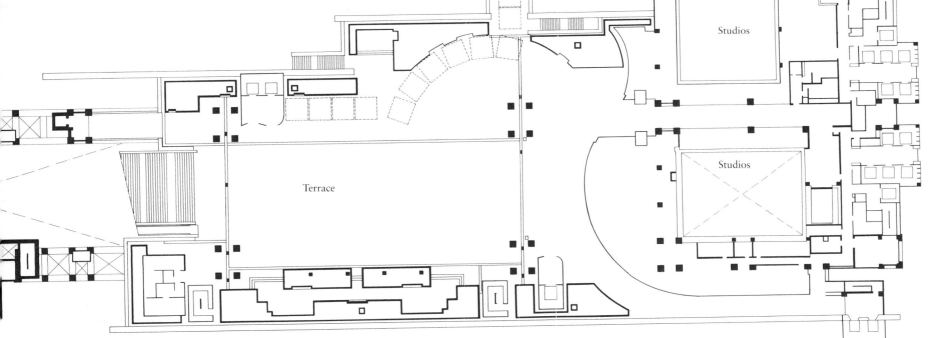

Itsuko Hasegawa

Born 1941
Education Kanto Gakuin University;
Tokyo Institute of Technology
Work Kiyonori Kikutake 1964–9;
Kazuo Shinohara Atelier 1971–8;
established Itsuko Hasegawa
Atelier 1979; lecturer Waseda
University 1988, Tokyo Institute
of Technology 1989–; visiting
professor Harvard Graduate
School of Design, US 1992
Major projects Shonandai Cultural Centre,
Fujisawa 1986
(1st prize, BCS prize)
Urban Scape, Shiogama 1989
(1st prize)
Nigita City Performing Arts Centre
and Area Development 1993
(1st prize)
Busshoji Elementary School 1993
Ohshimamachi Picture Book
Museum 1994
Museum of Fruit, Yamanashi 1995
University of Shiga Prefecture
Gymnasium 1995
Kurahashi-Machi Town Centre
and Area Development 1995
(1st prize)
Shiogama City Children's Centre
1995 (1st prize)
Himi Seaside Botanical Garden
1996
Kaiho Elementary School 1996
Prizes Architectural Institute of Japan
1986; Japan Cultural Design
Award 1986; Avon Arts Award
1990

Steven Holl

Born 1947
Education University of Washington;
Architectural Association, London,
UK
Work Established Steven Holl Architects
(New York) 1976; professor
Columbia University Graduate
School of Architecture and
Planning New York 1981–;
University of Washington; Pratt
Institute New York; University of
Pennsylvania Philadelphia
Major projects Pool House and Studio, Scarsdale,
New York 1981
Pace Collection Showroom, New
York 1985
Urban Proposal, Porta Vittoria
District, Milan, Italy 1986
Coop Renovation, Metropolitan
Tower, New York 1988
Hybrid Building Offices and
Condominiums, Seaside, Florida
1989
Apartment Building, Fukuoka,
Japan 1989
AGB Library, Berlin, Germany
1989 (1st prize)
Edge of a City Exhibition, Walker
Arts Center, Minneapolis 1989
Texas Stretto House, Dallas
1989–91 (National AIA Honor
Award for Excellence in Design)
Palazzo del Cinema, Venice, Italy
1990
Cranbrook Institute of Science,
Michigan 1991– (New York
Honor Award for Excellence in
Design)
Offices and Computer Equipment
Room, New York 1992 (National
AIA Interiors Award)
Makuhari Housing, Chiba, Japan
1992–6 (National AIA Honor
Award for Excellence in Design)
Museum of Contemporary Art,
Helsinki, Finland 1993– (1st
prize)
Urban Planning, Münich,
Germany 1994
Chapel of St Ignatius, Seattle,
Washington 1995– (New York

Honor Award for Excellence in
Design)
Prizes Arnold W. Brunner Prize for
Achievement in Architecture as an
Art, American Academy and
Institute of Arts and Letters 1990
Exhibitions Museum of Modern Art, New
York 1989; 'Architecture
Tomorrow', Walker Art Center
Minneapolis 1991
Publications Steven Holl, *Anchoring*, Princeton
University Press 1989; Stuart
Wrede (ed), *Emilio Ambasz/Steven
Holl: Architecture*, Museum of
Modern Art, New York 1989;
'Steven Holl', *GA Architect 11*
(8/93); 'Steven Holl', *Artemis*
(8/93); 'Steven Holl', *Archithese*
(3/94); Steven Holl, 'Questions of
Perception: Phenomenology of
Architecture', *A + U* 1994

Kouichi Sone

Born 1936
Education Tokyo University of Fine Arts
Work Established Kankyo Keikaku
Kenkyujo 1968
Prize Architectural Institute of Japan
Special Prize 1969

Toshio Enomoto

Born 1949
Education University of Tokyo
Work Core architect for Kajima Design
since 1972

Biographies

TAO Architects (Kimura Takeo)

Born 1949

Education Tokyo National University of Fine Arts; Rice University, Texas, US

Work Established TAO Architects with Shuntaro Noda 1981; lecturer Tama Art University 1984–9, Japan Women's University 1985, 1992, Musashino Art University 1996–

Major projects T House, Kanagawa 1981
T&K House, Tokyo 1985
Kosaka Head Office, Tokyo 1986
Nissei Life Plaza, Tokyo 1987
House in Yukigaya, Tokyo 1988
Jack in the Box House, Kanagawa 1989
Shukoh Head Office, Tokyo 1989
Gill (commercial), Tokyo 1991
K2 House, Shizuoka 1992
Sticks (office), Tokyo 1992

Prizes International Award for Innovative Technology in Architecture 'Quaternario 90' 1990; Housing Award sponsored by Shizuoka Prefecture 1993

Exhibitions 'Neo-Forma', Axis Gallery, Tokyo 1989; 'Invisible Language', Parsons School of Design, New York 1991 and Architectural Association, London 1992

Kenzo Tange

Born 1913

Education University of Tokyo

Work Established Kenzo Tange Associates 1961; professor University of Tokyo 1946–; visiting professor MIT, US 1959–60; visiting professor Harvard University, US 1972

Major projects Hiroshima Peace Centre 1949–55
Kurashiki City Hall 1958-60
A Plan for Tokyo 1960: Towards a Structural Reorganisation 1959–60
National Gymnasia for Tokyo Olympics 1961–64
St Mary's Cathedral, Tokyo 1961–64
Yamanashi Press and Broadcasting Centre, Tokyo 1961–7
Masterplan for Expo 70, Tokyo 1966–70
Kuwait International Air Terminal Building 1967-79
Bologna New Northern Development Project, Italy 1975–94
Central Area of New Federal Capital of Nigeria 1979–82
Hiroshima Culture Centre 1980–5
Japanese Embassy, Saudi Arabia 1982–5
Yokohoma Art Museum 1983–9
Singapore Indoor Stadium, 1985–9
Tokyo City Hall, 1985–91
Tokyo Plan (1960–86) 1986
Bay Square, Yokosuka 1989–93
Redevelopment Plan for the Left Bank, Paris, France 1990–93
Masterplan for EMI Administration Center, San Francisco, US 1991–3
Singapore Tele Tech Park 1994–

Prizes Royal Gold Medal, Royal Institute of British Architects 1965; Gold Medal, American Institute of Architects 1966; Grande Médaille d'or d'architecture, Académie d'Architecture, France 1973; Grand Prize, Architectural Institute of Japan 1986; Pritzker Architecture Prize, US 1987

Publications Kenzo Tange, *Katsura: Tradition and Creation in Japanese Architecture*, Yale University Press 1960; Kenzo Tange, *A Plan for Tokyo 1960: Towards a Structural Reorganization*, Shinkenchikusha, 1961; Robin Boyd, *Kenzo Tange*, George Braziller Inc. 1962; Kenzo Tange, *Ise: Prototype of Japanese Architecture*, MIT Press 1965; Udo Kultermann, *Kenzo Tange 1946–1969*, Artemis 1970; *Kenzo Tange*, Artemis (StudioPaperback) 1987; *Kenzo Tange 1946–1996*, Arnoldo Mondadori Editore 1996

●●●ellipsis

ellipsis specialises in publishing contemporary architecture and art and culture using a range of media, from books to the world wide web. Contact us for a copy of our pocket catalogue.

> ... earthier than Racine, more passionate than Stendhal, more encyclopaedic than Diderot and saucier than Escoffier.
> Hermine Poitou, INIT

A: 55 Charlotte Road London EC2A 3QT
E: ...@ellipsis.co.uk
W: http://www.ellipsis.co.uk/ellipsis
T: +44 171 739 3157
F: +44 171 739 3175

●●●electric editions

The ellipsis world wide web site is growing. It has been presented at numerous exhibitions and festivals, and the critics like it:

> ellipsis wins. It wins with creativity. It wins with content. It wins with innovation. You need to see this site, just to get a glimpse of what online publishing can do. The overall design pulls the surfer in and, with its intriguing graphical concepts, almost demands that s/he stick around for a while ... Users cruise through ellipsis pointing and clicking at icons that don't seem to make sense at first, since they rely heavily on intuitive action. But users 'learn by doing' what the different symbols and metaphors mean. It's a little complicated, but also challenging. The results are a joy to see.
>
> This is quite possibly one of the greatest web sites I have ever visited: ever-unfolding into interactive activity, a hyperlink game, and digital transcendence. This IS the place to be.
> BG, The Net magazine (USA)

The electric art cd-rom/book series was launched in March with Simon Biggs' *Book of Shadows*; number 2, *Passagen*, is due in Spring 97.

●●●paper editions

Our intention is always to publish in the most appropriate format – ranging from the interactive, intangible on-line pages of the world wide web, to the dual electronic and paper form of the electric art series, *Mekons United* with its book and audio cd, and conventional books.

These include Architecture in Context, books designed to appeal to anyone with an interest in contemporary building. The first four titles cover recent projects in Tokyo, Las Vegas, San Francisco, and Vienna. Essays provide the context necessary to understand the work – antecedents, functions, technology, urban issues – which is shown in specially commissioned photographs and drawings.

We have a paperback reprint of our very successful autobiography of Peter Rice, *An Engineer Imagines*, and a ground-breaking and very beautiful book on architecture and cyberspace, *Digital Dreams*. *The Internet and Everyone* is an important work by John Chris Jones, author of *Design Methods* and *Designing Designing*, in which he brings an unparalleled depth and range of thought to the information superhighway. Starting life on the internet, one stage of the work's development will be its existence as a book.

●●●architecture guides

> The best new guides to recent architecture are published by ellipsis.
> Colin Amery, The Financial Times

With a critical approach, an innovative, pocket-sized format, high-quality illustrations, and award-winning design, this series of guides – now available in English, German and French editions – describes and comments on significant contemporary architecture.

In preparation are books covering New York, San Francisco, Paris, Berlin, Sydney, Dublin, Madrid, Istanbul, Budapest, and Hong Kong, with still more to come.

Chicago: a guide to recent architecture
Susanna Sirefman

> ... should proved irresistible to architecture buffs.
> Chicago Herald Tribune
> ... the perfect yuppie travel companion ... discrete enough to refer to on the Loop, potted enough to do so between stops, detailed enough to impress and indiscrete enough to entertain.
> The Art Book Review Quarterly

England: a guide to recent architecture
Samantha Hardingham/photographs by Susan Benn

> Latest in a delectable series ... informative, opinionated, critical text; compact, sharply printed pix. Hardingham is a positive guide to the grand, the witty, the shoddy, the soaring, the sober, the dumb.
> The Observer
> ... remarkably up-to-date ... a fresh perspective is provided in the concise and spikily perceptive comments from the AA-trained author. The book is a pocket-sized bonus for the architecture-watcher.
> Paul Finch, The Architects' Journal

London: a guide to recent architecture
Samantha Hardingham

> ... positively plump with exploring zeal and opinion ... Truly pocket-sized and strongly recommended.
> The Observer
> ... it can only be applauded for broadening the audience for contemporary architecture and design.
> Lorenzo Apicella, Building Design

Las Vegas: a guide to recent architecture
Frances Anderton and John Chase/photographs by Keith Collie

This is the first guide to the architecture of Las Vegas. It describes and illustrates the casinos, the hotels, and the glorious lights and neon signage of the most popular gambling mecca in the world.

Los Angeles: a guide to recent architecture
Dian Phillips-Pulverman

In the second half of this century Greater Los Angeles has become a forcing ground for avant-garde architecture, and the appetite for experiment is as strong as ever. This book describes and illustrates more than 100 buildings completed over the last ten years.

Prague: a guide to twentieth-century architecture
Ivan Margolius/photographs by Keith Collie

> ... up-to-date and well worth reading ... An excellent small (in size), big (in content) guide which should decorate the shelf, or rather the pocket, of any interested architect.
> Robert Voticky, Building Design

Tokyo: a guide to recent architecture
Noriyuki Tajima/photographs by Keith Collie

> ... beautifully designed and illustrated ... Tajima's witty and enticing commentaries entice readers to make their own journeys of discovery.
> Joe LaPenta, The Daily Yomiuri

Vienna: a guide to recent architecture
Ingerid Helsing Almaas/photographs by Keith Collie

> ... that rarity – a guide-book that is a pleasure to read in full.
> The Architects' Journal

Mekons United

The Mekons were one of a group of bands to emerge from Leeds University/art school in the late 1970s. In the years since, the band has moved from punk through various musical styles, collaborated with dancers, artists and writers, and produced a stream of albums. In April 1996 an exhibition of Mekons art opened in Florida. This book presents a selection of that art, and includes a major essay by Terry Atkinson on the pop art explosion and the politics that led to punk, other essays on the economics of rock 'n' roll, the topography of Leeds, football and popular culture, art theory, and on the Mekons themselves.

The book also includes extracts from *Living in Sin*, the Mekons' novel in progress, with contributions from Kathy Acker, and a cd with more than an hour of previously unreleased Mekons music.

> *Mekons United* is a *tour de force* from perhaps the only band that exhibits equal ability in the musical and visual arts
> Chris Morris, Billboard

Digital Dreams: architecture and cyberspace
Neil Spiller

Architecture in crisis: the era of virtual reality, cyberspace, prosthetics and nano-technology. **Secrecy and experimentation – the fears and ecstasies of the painter; the drawing as a recording of the body's creative dance.** Exploring superspace as a series of perceptual frames or surfaces with intersecting boundaries. **Surface empathy is one of the conditions of being human.** Cyberspace is another realm of architectural opportunity. **Alchemy and its transformations parallel the emergent technologies of cyberspace, nano-technology and prosthetics.** The concept of the quantum smear (the ubiquity of the electron) leads to the idea of parallel universes and the infinite states of the object.

An Engineer Imagines
Peter Rice

Now in paperback, Peter Rice's autobiography is a personal account of the joy and enthusiasm he gave to and took from his profession. Rice was widely acclaimed as the greatest structural engineer of his generation, a man who, in Renzo Piano's words, could design structures 'like a pianist who can play with his eyes shut'.

> The book explains Rice's perception of, and contribution to, his most significant projects and lets the reader discover his very genuine humanity and concern for quality and sensuality. All concerned with these issues in our built environment should take the trouble to read it.
> Ian Ritchie, The Architects' Journal
> In *An Engineer Imagines*, the author accomplishes what was surely his principal reason for devoting his last year to this book: making vivid the process, excitement, and satisfactions of creative engineering.
> Joseph Passonneau, Architectural Record

Britain: a guide to architectural styles from 1066 to the present
Hubert Pragnell

> I have a friend who once asked for a list of architectural styles to pin up in her bathroom so that she could recite them every day as she prepared for the world. She worried that she did not know when the Romanesque ended and the Gothic began. Even more worrying for some is knowing what is going on in contemporary architecture. For instance, what is post-modernism all about?
> At last help is at hand ... Above all, this little book is for the beginner to take to the streets. Armed with its basics, they may find enough architectural pleasure to last a lifetime.
> Colin Amery, The Financial Times

The Art of the Structural Engineer
Bill Addis

Recognition of the structural engineer's contribution to building design has grown enormously in recent years. Rather than being seen as a sobering influence on the creativity of architects, daring and innovative engineers are rightly acknowledged as creators in their own right, exploring materials and structures as part of the design team.

> Engineers who read this book will come to understand architects better. It will help architects too, even if only to look at engineers in a kinder light.
> Will Howie, New Civil Engineer

The Internet and Everyone
John Chris Jones

how to improve the world without making matters worse

this is the architecture of living decentrally

:prelude:
Is there something that can be added now to the idea of the internet, and to its presence, that really improves industrial life, and culture? My first answer to this question, which I wrote as an outline of this book for ellipsis and McGraw Hill, was as follows:

...

Date Wed, 25 Oct 1995 02:07:19 +0100
To ...@ellipsis.co.uk
From jcj@ellipsis.co.uk
Subject the internet & everyone

dear tom & jonathan ... & everyone
OUTLINE OF THE IDEAS
When I think of the internet I realise that, though beginning as a special medium additional to others such as surface mail, phone, fax, radio, tv, etc, it is likely to grow rapidly as a general or meta-medium (as was print and the book) that legitimises and changes the forms of all the others.

What I will be writing is my long-held view that, as computation expands, all of the specialised departments of modern life, everything from government and education to medicine and show business, will have to undergo gradual but total change or transformation as the computernet and its possibilities, threatening and benign, provoke organisations and ordinary people to develop in extraordinary ways, many of them contradictory.

That is, I will suggest that there will evolve computernet-based versions of everything, very different from the present ones (which are based on the direct presence of people in specialised roles).

The central point of this view of things is that specialisation is no longer the right form for living in industrial culture. I believe that the logic of the change from mechanical to post-mechanical, via electronic media and computing, implies that people cease to organise themselves in specialised roles, as experts highly skilled in narrowband jobs. With the aid of a computerised internet, everyone should be able to take back (from what remains of the specialised professions) the creativeness and initiative that was long ago lost to them. As I see it, the presence of accessible computing power, embedded in everything, will turn the technical know-how of experts into accessible software and their manual skills and intuitions into the normal abilities of everyone else.

The obvious precedent for this is in the early days of writing and printing. Where once there were expert scribes and readers, able to write and to print what most people could only speak, there is now widespread literacy and the recent coming of self-publishing, by computer desk-top.

Equally relevant to this is the way in which the highly complex skills of speaking and listening to colloquial speech, still beyond the abilities of computers, are not beyond the immense abilities of every single person, the gifts we were all born with. And also the way in which languages grow and change spontaneously, in ways which baffle the so-called experts in language, but without any trace of central control or design or rule by specialists.

I believe that in the immediate future of the internet the question of whether it is to grow decentrally as it began, or under the central control which the media people and the corporations would like it to become, is a main question of the time. To me, nothing else matters as much, though I suppose that is crankiness, or fanaticism. (We have to go beyond that if the future is not to be a mess!)

My purpose in writing the book is to show in some detail exactly how it is that the old path (of expert centralism) is no longer right and that the new path (of what has been called creative democracy made possible by computernet) is the right way to go. Just because it's more human, in a way that primitive industrialism never was.

In this vision of universal change from centralism to its reverse, one or two things are essential: for example, how to let go and how to keep the centre empty.

But I've not got time at the moment to say any more than that.